A Harrowing Journey

Desiree Trattles

ISBN: 1502713543
ISBN-13: 978-15027113544

DEDICATION

I dedicate this book to Chris, my husband, my love, my best friend and my fellow traveller through times good and bad.

ACKNOWLEDGEMENTS

Writing a book is never a single-handed task, even in these days of self-publishing. I want to thank Peggy Naumann for her line-editing, encouragement and advice. I would like to thank Alan and Jane Mugglestone and Chris for their proof-reading work. I would also like to thank Dave Kitson for his help in producing a cover. And thank you for all of you out there who told me "Desi . . . write a book!"

CONTENTS

Foreword   7

Chapter 1   9

Chapter 2   15

Chapter 3   26

Chapter 4   31

Chapter 5   37

Chapter 6   41

Chapter 7   50

Chapter 8   54

Chapter 9   61

Chapter 10   70

Chapter 11   78

Chapter 12   84

Chapter 13   89

Chapter 14   94

Chapter 15   99

Chapter 16   104

Chapter 17   109

Chapter 18   116

Chapter 19   120

Chapter 20   125

Chapter 21   130

Chapter 22   135

Chapter 23   140

Chapter 24   144

Chapter 25   149

Chapter 26   154

Chapter 27   158

Chapter 28   162

Chapter 29   168

Chapter 30   172

Chapter 31   175

Chapter 32   180

Chapter 33   184

Chapter 34   189

Chapter 35   195

About the author   198

FOREWORD

What follows is a true story. It is what happened seen from my eyes. But, truth is a funny thing. The same event seen by other eyes can appear quite different. If you were there and have a different view of what happened, I acknowledge that your truth is as valid as mine. To protect the privacy of those involved in the convoy of 2011, I have changed the names of my fellow travellers and their boats. For the same reason, I do not include any photographs.

This is my story.

CHAPTER 1

I was dreaming of safety.

Oh, what heaven it would be just to feel safe again. I wanted it back. I wanted to be at peace, to sit in the cockpit at night and watch the stars and not feel that knot in my stomach. To just enjoy the sound of the seas slapping against the hull, as we made progress toward a safe harbour. I wanted to open my eyes and not be afraid of seeing a light in the distance. I wanted to sleep, sleep properly. That was the dream . . .

The reality, that night, was that I was on our small yacht, *Skylark II*, in the middle of the pirate-infested Indian Ocean. My husband, Chris, was asleep below while I was on watch, struggling to stay awake. Somewhere in the black of the night was one other small yacht, *Libertad*, and on board our travelling companions in this nightmare, Lucia and Juan. We were making our way from the Maldives to Yemen and were having to do it the long way, around the edges of the Indian Ocean, as going through the middle was too dangerous. The year was 2011 and Somali pirate activity was at an all-time high, with up to three attacks daily.

Beep! The watch alarm pulled me back into reality.

I reached for the black button, to reset it for fifteen minutes again, with my eyes still half closed.

Damn! I had almost drifted off! No, no, no! Mustn't do that! Must stay alert!

I forced my eyelids open and hauled myself up until I was standing in the cockpit, holding on to the roof of the dodger. I got on my knees on the cockpit seat and leaned my upper body outward, toward the starboard side deck, toward the black of the night, so that the cooling breeze on my face could wake me up properly. Fearfully, I looked around, trying to penetrate the absolute darkness around me.

Is there someone out there? I listened, knowing that the bad guys would not be showing me a light. Can I hear an outboard motor in the distance? No, I think not . . . Not this time.

I got up again and knelt on the port side this time.

Anything there? Where is *Libertad*? I should at least be able to see their faint light.

We were of necessity travelling without navigation lights: a no-no by international maritime law. But, out here, those laws did not apply. We were in the Indian Ocean, the domain of the Somali pirates. Out here you did anything you could, not to be seen. We were two small yachts amongst and against the multitude of pirates roaming this ocean. We stuck together and tried to be invisible. Our one concession to not losing each other's boats, in this vast ocean, was a small white light, encased in a black sock. We could just make each other's light out, if we were close enough. More than fifty metres away, and we would lose sight of one another.

Oh yes . . . There they are . . . just to my port and slightly behind.

Irrationally, that brought me some comfort. It was a false comfort. What on earth could any of us do if we were attacked?! Nothing, absolutely nothing! Juan and Lucia had weapons, it's true, but this actually put us into grave danger. The collective opinion of the yachties, and advice from the Coalition forces, was that whatever you do, "Don't offer resistance!"

It was better to accept your fate, put your hands up and hope not to be killed. Any kind of resistance would mean a gun battle and they would win. The pirates had Kalashnikovs, rocket propelled grenades, handguns, rifles . . . whatever . . . and they would not hesitate to use them. It would be an uneven battle and we would likely get killed in the crossfire.

So, Chris and I were not happy about the weapons on *Libertad*.

But, we did understand. Juan and Lucia came from South America where kidnapping and hostage-taking were commonplace. They had grown up on the horror stories of what happens to hostages. They were determined not to be captured, regardless of the cost. They would rather die than be captured.

We had not exactly planned to be travelling with a yacht that carried weapons but there was no point in thinking about that. Life had intervened in our lives again, turning our plans to custard. We thought we would be in the midst of a convoy of thirty boats; that's what we had signed up for. For various reasons, we had lost them all; all except *Libertad*. So, our choice was to stick with them or sail on alone. The thought of being alone, just us, by ourselves out here, was unthinkable. Even if there was no real advantage in being two boats, it did provide some moral support. I was truly terrified of losing them.

Well, nothing to be seen out here, I thought.

Beep!

There goes the watch alarm again. I'll go below now and check the radar.

We were so happy to have the radar. It had been a last minute addition, before embarking on this trip. We normally avoided collisions at sea by using AIS: automatic identification system. Ships would emit a signal, which our AIS would pick up, showing us where they were in relation to us. They could also see us in the same way, from the signal we were broadcasting.

But not out here, not in this ocean! We were not the only ones trying to be invisible. There were freight-ships out there . . . tankers . . . huge things . . . all trying to avoid capture by the pirates. Like us, they had also turned off their lights and their AIS and were travelling at top speeds to get out of that ocean. If we were unlucky enough to be run over by one of them in the night, they would probably not even know that they had hit us. They might find bits of rigging entangled in their bows when they got to the next port.

"Oh whoops!! Must have hit some unlucky bastard!" It happens . . . more often than you think. It wasn't just pirates we were afraid of!

Must stay alert.

There was no point in thinking about possible collisions.

Nothing we can do about it, except try to stay alert and hope to see their shadow, before they get too close.

Must stay alert! Must stay alert! Must stay alert!

I was so tired, so exhausted. We had been on this ocean for weeks, almost a month. There was no respite from the anxiety, the fear. I couldn't remember the last time that I had a good night's sleep. We had spent almost that entire time out at sea, doing watches, so even if I had been able to shut out the constant conversation in my head, the longest stretch we could sleep was three or four hours. The lack of sleep was taking its toll. I was ill. I was feverish and in the grips of a bad case of bronchitis. I had lost my voice, almost completely. But, there was no time for that.

I couldn't say "Sorry Chris . . . I'm not feeling well . . . think I'll take a break for a couple of days!" There were just the two of us, and he was every bit as tired and terrified as I was. There was nothing to do but carry on, carry on, carry on.

Beep! went the watch alarm again.

Oh yes, I was going to check the radar.

Must stay alert!

I went below to the nav table and flicked on the radar screen. We kept it on standby the whole time . . . Sod the energy drain! My eyes adjusted to the picture. I scrolled the range in and out, first close by, then further away from us.

There is the dot that signifies *Libertad.* Good! They are where I expected them to be. But hang on . . . What the hell is that?

I could feel myself tense as I stared at another blob on the screen . . . a target . . . in radar-speak.

Shit!!! I moved the cursor to draw a line from the middle of the radar, which depicted where we were, and the target. It was fairly close, and what's more, it was heading straight for us!!! It was a smallish target. Not as big as a tanker or large freight ship; but bigger than a yacht, bigger than *Libertad's* blob.

A smallish freight ship then? *Mother ship! Mother ship! Mother ship!!!* went through my head.

Quickly, alert Juan and Lucia! I thought.

They did not have radar, so we were their eyes in the dark. We also did not dare use our normal means of inter-ship communication, the VHF radio. That had been banned ages ago, because anyone within a hundred miles who had a VHF receiver could hear you, including the pirates. Instead, we had devised a system, by which we would whistle into the VHF, using a channel that was not commonly in use. The other boat would acknowledge by a responding whistle. Then we would both go down below and turn on our ham radios to an agreed frequency and communicate on that. There are thousands of channels used on ham radio, so it would be very unlucky if the pirates were listening in.

"*Libertad, Libertad* . . . Juan . . . are you there?" I managed to squeak with my failing voice.

"Yes, go ahead, Desiree," came Juan's tired reply.

"Small target on radar, two miles away, heading directly toward us, very rapidly!" I squeaked.

"Ok!" He sounded more awake now. "Let's turn forty degrees to starboard and increase speed!"

"Roger that!" I replied. "I will turn forty degrees to starboard and increase speed!"

I leapt into the cockpit and quickly changed our heading on the autopilot by forty degrees. Then I upped the revs on the motor to 2600, the maximum we wanted to push our motor. Luckily the engine was already on. Lately we had motor-sailed most of the time, to make max speed and just get the hell out of that ocean.

I peered into the dark, in the direction of the oncoming ship. I could not see anything, only black night. The ship obviously had no lights on, or I would have seen something by now. I saw that Juan had turned off even the light in the sock, so I did the same.

Oh, please! Please let them not see us!

My stomach was now a tight knot. I felt like I might need to throw up.

Should I wake Chris? I wondered. He was still sleeping down

below, oblivious to the potential danger.

No . . . I'll leave him. There is nothing he can do . . . If we get caught, we get caught.

Nervously I gripped the "tiki" around my neck, a greenstone charm, given to us by a Maori friend when leaving New Zealand. "For luck." We were not normally especially superstitious, but out there, all bets were off. Whatever might give you even the tiniest edge!

I leaned down and glanced at the radar again.

Bloody hell . . . They are almost on top of us!

Just as I was thinking that, the dark night was lit up by a powerful spotlight. It swept an arc over the sea, just missing the back of our boat. I held my breath, my heart pounding in my ears!

This is it! This is really it! They are going to find us!

Sure enough, the spotlight swept the sea again . . . and this time . . . it shone straight into my eyes. I froze . . . like a rabbit in the headlights of a car. My mind went blank with fear.

Then *BOOM!* And the night had turned into broad daylight! I was completely confused.

What just happened?

Then it dawned on me. An illuminating flare! They have fired off an illuminating flare! To see us better! But . . . hang on . . . that does not sound like pirates?! That is more like something a navy vessel would do, surely? Perhaps these are the good guys . . . not the pirates?

Apparently, Juan had thought the same thing. He later told me that this had terrified him even more . . . He thought, *What if they think we are pirates and fire at us?!*

The flare died out, leaving us in darkness again, and like the flare, the drama soon fizzled.

Our two boats continued on the new course for a while and the radar showed the unknown ship moving off, away from us. This confirmed it . . . It had been a Coalition forces vessel of some kind and they had recognised that we were two small yachts. I started to breathe again.

Half an hour later, we resumed our original course. This time we had been lucky. I sat back exhausted and tried to regain what equilibrium I had left.

Is this ever going to end? I thought. I have had enough!

But, we were still miles from safety, weeks from safety . . . and there was nowhere to go . . . but on. We had really painted ourselves into a corner. I did not know it at the time, but there was worse to come. At that moment all I could wonder was how on earth it had all happened. How had we gotten ourselves into this mess? It had all started so benignly . . .

CHAPTER 2

As I sat in the cockpit that night, contemplating how we had ended up in such a mess, I thought back to the beginnings of our journey.

This particular leg of the journey had started in Thailand, but really . . . the path we were on, which had brought us to this particular moment, had started much, much earlier.

Where does a journey like ours actually start? There could be many starting points.

You could say the journey started four years earlier in May 2007 when we left the shores of New Zealand. Or you could say it started in January of 2006, when we left our home port of Mana. Or you could say that it started in December of 2005, when Chris finally retired. Or you could say that it started when we bought the boat in October 2002.

I like to think that the journey actually started on the day that we conceived of it . . . on the day that we brought together vague notions that it would be nice to retire and sail off into the sunset, and actually decided that we would make it happen. We would take this pipe dream, convert it into a real dream, take the real dream and convert it into a goal, and then do whatever it took to make that goal a reality. This took place a good ten years before final departure from New Zealand. We conceived of a ten year plan to make our dreams come true.

Now, you have to know . . . Chris and I are very ordinary people.

Somehow there is this misconception that people who are floating out there, retired and cruising the oceans, have to be independently wealthy in some way. That has certainly not been our experience. You meet people from all walks of life who are sailing the world. Yes, there are retired doctors, surgeons, airline pilots, and people who were just born with a silver spoon in their mouth. They are the exception. The vast majority come from more humble backgrounds. There are miners, schoolteachers, artists, divers, ex-military people, and small business owners. They come from all over the world, speak all sorts of languages, and believe in all sorts of things.

However, there is one thing they all have in common. A thirst for adventure, a passion for travel, a curiosity of what lies beyond their comfort zone . . . and the willingness to sacrifice some of the comforts and security of life on shore in order to pursue their passions. A willingness to throw yourself out into the vast unknown and see where you land. In short, cruisers are probably, in the eyes of those they have left behind . . . slightly nuts.

It has to be said, there are also a fair few unwilling participants out there on the ocean. I guess it is hard to find the passions that I have just described in equal measure in a marriage or partnership. In many, many cases, it is the husband, the male partner who dreams of a retirement on a boat. His wife is cajoled, caressed, bowled over with convincing arguments, and sometimes even bullied into the life at sea. Her ties lie on the land, with her children, her grandkids. I don't want to stereotype, but it is a reality that I have time and time again encountered women on boats who would rather be elsewhere. Not always though. I have certainly also met women who are passionate about the cruising life. There are even women who sail the world alone or who own and skipper their own boat and who take crew as needed. They are, to me, awe-inspiring, but they are the exception, not the rule.

Forgive me, if I interrupt myself . . . but . . . I have to tell you about Bridget!

We met her in Phuket, Thailand, and I had kind of heard about her through the grapevine. At the time we met her, she was boat-less but desperate to get out there again in a floating home. We invited her and her partner for a weekend on *Skylark*.

She told me her story one hot moonlit night, when we couldn't sleep and both ended up taking some fresh air on the foredeck.

Bridget had sailed many miles, many years with her husband and kids. They sailed as a family and pretty much brought up their three daughters on board. The daughters were now ten, fourteen and eighteen and they had decided to take them home to New Zealand to attend land based schools.

They were in the Canary Islands and about to cross the Atlantic. At the time they were sailing in company with some other yachts. Anyway, within hours of leaving the Canary Islands for the three thousand mile crossing to the Caribbean, Bridget's husband and lifetime partner collapsed on deck and died. I can't remember if it was a stroke or a heart attack, but . . . he died . . . just like that.

A mayday call summoned a helicopter and uplifted her husband. Bridget turned the boat around and headed back to the Canary Islands.

For most of us, that would have been it. We would have succumbed to our grief, sold the boat, packed up the kids and headed for home.

Not Bridget.

One night, a few days later, unable to sleep, she was sitting in the cockpit when an idea leapt to mind. They had been on their way back to New Zealand with their floating home. That was the plan, and that is what she would do.

She called the girls to a conference and said "What do you think, girls? Can we do it on our own?"

They agreed, and so they set to work to get ready to continue the journey.

Now . . . Bridget knew a lot about sailing their boat . . . but there were still things that her husband had always done. Those things that we cruising women call the "Blue Jobs." Engines are generally a "Blue Job," as are blocked toilets. Cooking and cleaning and laundry are "Pink Jobs," and those she already knew how to do.

Now she had to familiarize herself with the bits of the boat that her husband had handled.

She recruited the help of other cruisers to teach her and the children sail handling, engine maintenance and navigation. All went well without major hiccups. However, she recalled that at their first port of call, a crowded anchorage in the Cape Verde Islands, as they came in to anchor she realised she had no idea how to use the windlass to drop the anchor. Luckily friends were already waiting in the bay and at a panicked call on the VHF they leapt on board to help get the anchor down.

Anyway, this brave woman and her teenage daughters sailed their boat thousands of miles across the Atlantic, through the Caribbean to Panama, through the Panama Canal, through the South Pacific islands and finally to New Zealand. I think they arrived in New Zealand roughly a year after losing her husband and their father.

Hearing her story, I was humbled. I can't begin to imagine the courage it takes to pick yourself up off the floor, dust yourself off, and take on the challenges that the sailing life throws at you when you have just had the love of your life and your greatest support and comfort ripped away from you. I was in awe of her.

Funny thing though, she did not see herself as some kind of hero and was quick to point out that her girls played a major role in sailing the boat. She just "did what had to be done."

But then, heroes always say that . . . don't they?

But, where was I?

Oh yes . . . I was philosophizing about the start of our journey.

I think I'd come to the conclusion that our journey started at least ten years before we left New Zealand shores. And it did. Our lives changed significantly, once we made the decision to make it happen. We went out and told people we would do it.

"We are going to retire early and sail around the world . . . well not around the world perhaps . . . but a lot of it anyway!"

That was important . . .to say it out loud. To establish it as a fact.

"We are going to do this!"

Now there was accountability. We had said we would . . . so we'd better.

The challenge seemed huge. We were, as I mentioned, ordinary people.

We had good but not super-lucrative jobs. Chris was services engineer for the local Council in charge of water and sewage for the Kapiti Coast District Council. I was a newly fledged chartered accountant, having gone back to school "in-me-old-age" for a second career. (I was in my forties then.) I was working for KPMG in Wellington on a decent, but not huge, wage.

We had a house, partly paid off, but still with a bit of a mortgage on it. We had a camper van and a car but no boat. Oh . . . I lie . . .we had a small inflatable dinghy with a 2.5 horsepower outboard, which just fit into the camper van so we could putter about on a lake here and there. We had the ordinary household stuff, but . . . no savings to speak of.

The start of our planning went like this.

Let's see . . . what do we need to make our dream come true?

We need a boat . . . a sizeable one. That would probably cost us NZ$100,000–$150,000, even second hand.

We would need to equip it for long distance cruising . . . maybe another $50,000?

Oh yes . . . and we would need to put aside enough savings capital to generate a decent living for when we weren't working.

Let's see . . . if we can live on NZ$1,500 a month . . . after all, out there we won't have electricity bills, rates, car, etc . . . only food and the odd wrinkled T-shirt to worry about . . . Okay, so . . . if we can live on $1,500 a month, then savings of $150,000 might do it.

I know . . . you can't expect ten percent interest.

However, we had another small, but important, card up our sleeve. Chris was due a small private U.K. pension which we thought we might be able to cash in early. On the other hand, we could not count on any government pensions, as we would be too young to be eligible for these. (Chris ended up retiring at fifty-six and I was forty-nine.)

Either way, we had to somehow come up with a sizeable chunk of cash in the next ten years. We needed to *focus*.

Well, if I may pat myself on the back a little bit here, there was one thing that Chris and I were really good at. It was *Focus*.

For the next ten years we did nothing but work toward our goal. It was fun, in a way, even though we had to sacrifice a lot of present for the future. We hunkered down; you know . . . head down, bum up . . . and worked all hours that God sent. We had our jobs, and when we were not working on them, we started a direct sales business in our spare time. Regular jobs in the daytime. Nights and weekends on our business. Whenever we were tempted to stray and spend money on *other things* . . . we remembered the dream. Even birthday gifts and Christmas gifts had to do with the boat. I bought Chris a set of binoculars for one birthday. They are still with us today on board, but predate the boat by several years.

Along the way, our mortgage got paid off, and we decided to swap the house for the boat. We thought we'd spend a lot of time looking for a suitable boat. After all, we were not in a hurry. We still had four years to go before our planned retirement.

However, when you fall in love, you fall in love.

We had looked at only three other boats when we stumbled upon *Skylark II*. She wasn't even on the market at the time and had her owners living on board, but the boat broker had us figured out, and thought she might be "the one," and he was right.

Skylark II is a Shearwater 39. She is designed by a prolific South African designer called Dudley Dix and she is the only Shearwater ever built in aluminium. She was built in Cape Town for her first owner, a tall farmer called Lofty Huyshammer. We think he was tall because he specified extra headroom, and we think he was a farmer because her engine was a marinised tractor engine. She is a cutter rigged sloop, which means she has a single mast and can accommodate two head sails.

But . . . we did not fall in love with her because of her pedigree; in fact, we had never heard of the design or the designer before. Only later were we to find out that Shearwaters are very highly thought of by cruisers in the know. There are only a couple of dozen of them available worldwide, and they are sought after. We had stumbled upon a gem.

From first glance, we really loved everything about her, especially the open plan accommodation. She was light and airy inside with five great big hatches and a very roomy, comfortable cockpit. She had lots of varnished wood inside but none outside, which would make her easier to maintain. And she was metal. We wanted metal, so that if, or when, we bumped into a reef, we would hopefully get a dent rather than a hole. So, we were looking for either a steel boat or an aluminium one. Steel was much cheaper, but we were reluctant because of the constant fight with rust that comes with steel boats. We really, really wanted aluminium, but thought we would not be able to afford it. And sure enough, *Skylark II* was over our budgeted limit.

We got off the boat and walked down the dock. We looked at each other and said *"Shit!!!"*

That was all the commentary that was necessary. We both knew that this was our boat and that we would move mountains to get her.

We have never regretted that decision. *Skylark* has been absolutely wonderful to us. She has been all that we hoped for and more!

But we now had a little problem. The house was on the market but was not sold yet. We had to get bridging finance to get the boat and then hope the house sold in a hurry. The plan was to sell the house, then bring the boat down from her present location in Auckland to Mana, near Wellington, which was the marina closest to our jobs. This was quite a sail down a fairly treacherous coast. We would need crew, as there was no autopilot installed.

No problem, some friends could help.

We would do it over the Christmas break. We would drive up to Auckland in our camper van, because there would be a lot of household stuff to bring along. We would then hand over the camper van to some friends who wanted to borrow it for three months and tour the North Island. Once the boat was in Mana, we could take our time and slowly move onto the boat. Then the house would sell and we would pay back the bridging finance. It would all work out wonderfully well.

Yeah right. Not!!!

A week before our departure with the camper van to Auckland to get the boat, our broker told us the house was sold and the new owners wanted to move in the first week of January.

Yikes!

We had a week to get rid of all that we owned in the house, because we would not be back in time with the boat before the owners took possession.

No problem.

We quickly put together invitations for a house-emptying sale for that weekend, and handed them out at work and to local friends. On the day, we handed each person a list with all our furniture and appliances and encouraged them to make a bid for whatever they wanted. At the end of the day, the person with the highest bid would take the item.

It worked beautifully. By the end of the day we had gotten rid of eighty percent of our possessions.

Items of sentimental value were packed into boxes for storage, as were things we thought we might need on the boat.

A week later, we locked the doors of our now empty house, got in the camper van and set off for the next phase in our lives.

Now, I can hear some of you thinking . . . I could never do that! I love my house too much; I love my stuff.

We are not cold hearted. We loved our house a lot. In fact, it had also been love at first sight, almost the same feeling as when we saw *Skylark* for the first time. I admit that there were feelings of uncertainty when we closed that door, when we watched people walk off with our furniture and possessions.

But the feeling of impending adventure was stronger. We knew all along, that to fulfil our dream, sacrifices would be required of us. This was one of them and, after all, stuff is just that, stuff. It was replaceable, and what was not, would be waiting for us in storage.

A couple of months later, when we were already living on the boat in Mana, Chris asked me whether I missed our beloved house. I thought about it and had to admit that I did not.

"I sometimes miss the Jacuzzi," I replied.

He said "Hang in there. Soon you will have the biggest Jacuzzi in the whole world, all around the boat."

So, the house was gone. We headed to Auckland in the camper van to pick up the boat. As planned, we handed the camper van over to friends and wished them *"Bon voyage."* We then spent the next couple of weeks familiarizing ourselves with *Skylark II*. Chris' son Simon and my sister Pakeezah had arrived from abroad and we had a wonderful first cruise with them in the Hauraki Gulf.

Soon enough the gentle cruise was over, and it was time to face the sometimes ferocious east coast of New Zealand, in order to get the boat down to its new home port.

We weren't really ready. The boat was very new to us and ill equipped. For instance, there was no light on the compass, so at night we would have to shine a torch on the compass to see where we were going. We had no life raft, no autopilot . . . Well, there were a bunch of things we did not have. We did decide to buy a parachute anchor, just in case.

Son Simon was dispatched back to the UK, but sister Pakeezah pleaded to come along on the delivery. I explained to her that this was not likely to be a champagne cruise. There was the very real possibility that we could end up in rough weather.

"You don't have the experience," I said.

In the end, she insisted. And we were glad she did, as she ended up cheering all us "experienced" sailors up when it got horrible.

Our chosen crew for the trip were good friends, Roger and Otto. They were both leaders of the Wellington Sea-Scouts and Roger was a former harbour pilot, with a yacht of his own.

It started well. We left Auckland and headed around toward the East Cape. The plan was to round the Cape and then head down the Wairarapa Coast, through Cook Strait and slightly north to Mana. The trip would take about a week, maybe less.

Now, those of you who know anything about sailing in New Zealand would know that all the locations I mentioned above are notorious for potential bad blows. The East Cape is famous for something called "The River of Wind" which comes down from the high cliffs and whips up the sea into a frenzy. To make matter worse, two sets of waves moving in different directions meet at the Cape, and this combination of rough seas and lots of wind can make for some challenging sailing.

And that's what happened!

We ended up in very bad winds trying to round the Cape. The first night we tried to wait it out by heading into a bay, but found we were tacking back and forth and barely making headway. Then we blew out the mainsail.

Now, we were handicapped.

We also started to hear a strange vibrating sound that seemed to come from the propeller shaft. Not good!

We found ourselves in big waves just off the Cape as nightfall was approaching. Roger and Otto handed over the watch to Chris and me. It was all we could do to keep the boat headed into the wind and waves. It was important to stay head to the waves or we would be in danger of broaching, that is, the boat could end up sideways to the seas and be rolled by them. It was getting darker and darker and Chris and I realised that we would soon be struggling with lighting the compass with the torch as well as trying to hold the boat into the wind. It would be too much. Chris made the decision to put the boat on parachute anchor.

A parachute anchor is just that, a large parachute (ours is five metres in diameter), that you deploy in the water. It is attached by a long line to the bows of the boat and acts like a big brake, holding the boat head to the wind. You still drift, as you are not attached to the bottom, but you drift slowly, very slowly, backwards. It means that you can stop sailing and wait out the weather.

That was the theory.

The parachute anchor was still in its plastic wrapping. We had not even unpacked it. Chris sat in the cockpit and quickly read the instructions while we did our best to follow them.

It worked like a charm. One minute, all was havoc, wind and waves throwing the boat around; the next minute there was calm. Sure, there were still wind and waves and the boat danced back and forth a bit on the bowline, but we were no longer crashing into the waves. The waves were now approaching us directly from the bows and harmlessly passing underneath the boat. We could stand upright, make coffee, take a nap, or just think.

We spent the night like that, on the parachute anchor. We still had to keep an anchor-watch and look out for other ships in the night. If one approached, we needed to warn them that we were there and could not get out of their way. But there were no ships that night. No one else was foolish enough to be out in that kind of weather. We kept contact with a Coast Guard station on land not far away. The operator tried to cheer us up and commiserate while he sat there in the warm and dry with his cup of coffee.

Dawn arrived, but the wind had not abated. We discussed what to do. As we now had no mainsail, we agreed that it would be foolish to continue down the coast. We would have to retreat back to the nearest large port, which was Tauranga.

However, getting off a parachute anchor once it is deployed is not an easy thing. You have to motor up to a float, which is attached to a trip line. The trip line, once pulled on board, will deflate the parachute and allow you to pull it in. The problem is, that to approach this float, you are heading into the lines attached to the parachute. If one of those goes around the propeller, you could be in big trouble. It is a tricky operation and best attempted once the storm has passed and the waves died down.

For us, there was another issue. We did not know how the boat handled. Motoring up to the float could put us parallel to the waves.

Would she ride over them . . . or would she lose her balance and fall off the edge of a wave into a broach?

We just did not know. A broach would not sink her, but it might mean a few broken ribs or other damage to the crew. A third consideration (which should never be a consideration when at sea) was that the crew, and us, had only a limited time for this delivery. People couldn't hang out there forever. They had lives and jobs to get back to.

In the end, we decided to try it.

Skylark was a champ! We did end up side-to the waves but she just bobbed gracefully over them. No problem at all!

We retrieved the parachute and headed downwind toward Tauranga.

Our entrance into the harbour was a rollercoaster ride. As we approached shore, the huge waves got bigger and bigger. The boat was surfing down them at great speed. To make matters worse, there was a heavy fog. We could see nothing of the shore until we were almost upon the narrow harbour entrance. In this situation Roger was worth his weight in gold. As a harbour pilot, he had previously guided ships into this narrow entrance.

He put Chris on the helm and everyone else below and told Chris, "Do exactly as I say!"

With gritted teeth, Chris followed his lead and we popped into that harbour like a champagne cork flying out of a bottle! Wow! Quite a start to our maritime adventures!

That day our crew departed for their homes in Wellington, and a few days later, Pakeezah was dispatched back to Auckland to catch her flight home.

Pakeezah was on a real high. To her innocent eyes, this had all been a tremendous adventure. I don't think she had any inkling how serious the situation potentially had been. In the midst of the storm, with the rest of us feeling pretty nervous and seasick, she had been a bundle of smiles, happily cooking up spaghetti which we were all rather too green to eat.

Chris and I now faced further problems. We also had jobs to get back to and little time, but we had to find someone to repair the sail, fix the rattle in the propeller shaft (it was misaligned), and to eventually deliver the boat to us, as we had run out of vacation time to do it ourselves. The cheques seemed to be flying out the door faster than I could sign them. Still, we left *Skylark* in capable hands and returned to Wellington.

Back home, still a bit shell-shocked, we thought about how our lives had already changed. Before Christmas, we had had a house and camper van in Wellington and a boat in Auckland. Now, we found ourselves with a boat in Tauranga (four hundred kilometres away), a camper van tiki-touring around the North Island somewhere . . . and no house. We were, in essence, homeless!

Boy-oh-boy! You can be certain that the "dream-stealers" loved that one!

I don't know how many people commiserated with us over this while they were probably secretly really, really pleased.

See what happens when you follow crazy notions to sail off into the sunset?, they thought. See what happens when you give up your home and security for some pipe dream?

In the end someone took pity on us and asked us to house-sit for them for a couple of weeks. This led on to another house-sitting job. By then, our friends who had borrowed the camper van had heard about our misadventure and returned the van to us early.

So we moved into the camper van. All in all, I think we were homeless for about six weeks.

At the end of that, the delivery crew of three orchard owners from Tauranga sailed *Skylark* down the coast to Mana.

It was an incredible feeling to see our new home coming over the Mana sandbar!

Dream-stealers, eat your heart out!

Our departure was still four years away, but we were now living on our boat!

CHAPTER 3

The years went by and we continued to *focus, focus, focus*. Every spare penny went into a growing stock portfolio, and at the time the market was in our favour, so the money started to grow.

We prepared in other ways too. Both Chris and I had done quite a bit of sailing before, but we had never taken any formal qualifications. We now rectified that by taking courses in seamanship and navigation. We also got very interested in self-improvement. We knew that we would spend years in very close proximity to one another. We reckoned that it would be wise to sort out any issues that we might have with one another, before we set off. So we started to attend various self-improvement courses.

Personally, I worked very hard at the self-improvement. I did feel that I succeeded in leaving behind a lot of baggage.

I had a rather turbulent past. I grew up in a home with an alcoholic father whom I nevertheless adored, and a self-absorbed mother who tended to forget that she had kids. Eventually there was divorce and a young stepmother, not many years my senior. We moved around a lot. I went to eight different schools before completing high school. Then Dad died of alcohol-related causes, when I was in my early twenties. I have sometimes described my growing up years as "living in a hurricane."

You can get addicted to that type of life though, and I continued the "hurricane" by getting into a rollercoaster relationship, which ended in tears. Many tears. A year after the end of that fifteen year relationship, my ex died, which I took very hard, even though I had by then started a new relationship with Chris.

I had a lot of demons, a lot of baggage. And, like my father, I tried to drown my sorrows, tried to find peace . . . in a bottle.

The self-development courses did help to deal with a lot of the causes of my drinking . . . or at least . . . the reasons that I used as excuses for my drinking. But the drinking did not stop. I was, by now, addicted to alcohol. I used to tell myself that I just needed to have a drink to smooth out the rough edges. Have a cold? Take a drink. You'll feel better. Had a rough day at work? Have a drink. You'll feel better. Had a success at work? Have a drink. Time to celebrate. Hate housework? Have a drink. It will be more fun then. The truth is, I would use any excuse at all to have a drink.

Now, I can hear you thinking . . . Wait a minute....This is the same person who is *focused, focused, focused* on this big adventure? Holding down a good job in order to make money to go sailing? This is the person who is about to take on momentous challenges that will try her resolve and mental stability?

Yep, the very one. I had a secret . . . a very heavy secret . . . I was an alcoholic.

And, it was a secret. Most alcoholics find that once they stop drinking they find out that what they thought was a secret drinking habit was actually common knowledge. Everyone knew. In my case it did not work out like that. When I finally came "out of the closet" pretty much everyone was gob-smacked. Sure, some people knew I liked a drink or two, but no one had suspected the scale of it.

Not even Chris. He did know I had a problem, but even he did not know how bad a problem.

I hid it well. I played all the little games common to the alcoholic. In the morning, I used to sneak a quick vodka . . . *to make my hands stop shaking*. Then I ate mints and went to work. By noon, I would start to feel ill again. Another small drink was required. So, I drove to the local KFC drive-through and ordered a chicken thigh and a diet coke. The diet coke would be spiked with a little vodka, *to make me feel better*. More mints. Back to work. At after-work parties I would nurse a glass of white wine all evening, but I'd be hanging out to get home for a proper drink.

My drinking was never in pubs or in public, nor was it at parties. I was morbidly afraid of letting others see my problem. I drank alone, at home, in secret. I drank vodka, because it has no odour. I went to a series of different liquor stores to buy my booze, being careful not to go to the same one too often, so they would not suspect that I had a habit. I hid my empties carefully and went to the recycling station very early in the morning when no one else was there. I sent Chris to the parking lot or the store, so I could have a quick drink on the boat while he was gone.

It was time-consuming and soul-destroying. I was lying to the people I cared about the most.

In September of 2003, Chris and I flew to the UK for the wedding of his son (my stepson) Nik. It was a huge family affair and we would be staying in the family home along with other relatives.

For weeks before our departure, I was obsessed with how I was going to handle my drinking habit, while surrounded by so many others. As for the flight . . . would I cope with a drink or two on the plane all the way to England?

The whole of the wedding was coloured by my obsession with this secret drinking. I ended up getting up at crack of dawn, when all the others were asleep. I would steal into the kitchen, grab a teacup and fill it with neat vodka from the freezer. With hands shaking so bad that I had to hold the cup with both hands, I stood by the fridge, paranoid at getting caught, and downed the vodka.

Problem was, I could see myself, like in a mirror, doing this. There I was . . . no doubt at all . . . full blown alcoholic! There was no escaping that image in the mirror.

I succeeded most days in finding an excuse to buy vodka.

"Lots of people around for the wedding!" I said "Got to make sure we have something to offer them to drink!"

However, the day came when I was out of booze. Like most good alcoholics, I had long since sussed out where my father-in-law kept his liquor. He had a single bottle of Chivas Regal which someone had given him years ago. He would maybe take a tot or two for Christmas. Whiskey was not my drink . . . but needs must . . . I "borrowed" his Chivas. But . . . that mirror which seemed to be following me around . . . did not agree.

"You are stealing whiskey from your ninety year old father-in-law!" the mirror said.

The wedding over, we flew back to New Zealand. I was totally disgusted with myself. I was fed up, fed up, fed up. I was fed up with being fed up!

I went on one last binge over the weekend and woke up on Monday morning, unable to go to work. I felt like death warmed over . . . a feeling that was becoming far too familiar. I was also scared. I was forty-eight years old and my father had killed himself due to alcohol at forty-nine. I had so much to live for . . . a wonderful loving husband . . . this huge adventure ahead of us. Was I going to ruin it all?

I picked up the phone and dialled my doctor. I made an appointment a couple of hours later. Then I phoned Chris at work and told him that I was going to see my doctor and confess that I was an alcoholic.

Chris said "I will cancel all my appointments and meet you there."

I'm so glad he did. If he had not, I am not sure that I could have gone through with it. I might have wiggled out, taken another drink, been back at square one. It was October the 7th, 2003 and I had taken my last drink.

What followed was a time of hardship, but also joy, relief, rebirth. The doctor said I had to go to a rehabilitation clinic for two months.

"No way! I am a manager. I have a responsible job. I have staff.

I can't just go away for two months! What will I say? What will people think?!"

Chris said, "You must do what they say. They know best. After all, you have not succeeded with dealing with this yourself. Now you must follow the advice of those who are experienced in dealing with alcoholism."

He was right. I knew he was. So . . . straight from the doctor's office I asked to be taken to my work place. I called my boss and the HR manager.

I said "I don't know how else to put this. Here it is. I am an alcoholic and have to go to rehab."

Their jaws dropped. They really had no inkling. They were also incredibly supportive. "Tell us how we can help."

I needed a week to dry out. I got it. No question. On full pay.

In the meantime, I started to see an alcohol counsellor and was referred to a rehabilitation clinic. I had to wait several weeks before I was admitted. So in the meantime I went back to work. Finally, it was time to go to rehab. My manager suggested I tell my staff that I had to take a couple of months off "for personal reasons" and leave it at that. However, I was fed up with telling lies and knew that there would be speculation about the nature of these "personal reasons." I called a staff meeting.

I will never forget that day. It was one of the hardest things I have ever done.

Once everyone was seated around the meeting room table I said "There is no pretty way to say this. I am an alcoholic. I will be leaving you for two months to attend rehab. Please do not lie on my behalf. Please don't volunteer the information, but if someone asks, you may tell them the truth."

There was silence in the room. No one said a word.

I said "That's all" and got up.

I returned to my desk and just sat there, humiliated, frightened, and scared. There was complete silence in our usually noisy office.

Then a *Pling*! I had received an email. It said "Good on you! My brother was an alcoholic. I am proud of you."

More emails followed and then people started to come up to my desk. The message was the same. "My brother, my mother, my uncle, my aunt."

It seemed everyone had someone close to them that had a problem. They were all surprised at my confession, but so happy for me that I was going to do something about it. I was truly humbled that day and have kept all those emails . . . so that I never forget. They threw a party for me on the day of my departure, with non-alcoholic wine and a cake. They wrote communal letters to me while I was away. I will never forget the kindness and support that I was given in those dark days. I have never taken a drink again.

CHAPTER 4

We were still two years away from our intended retirement date when I stopped drinking. We had decided to stop working at the very latest end of 2005. We made up our minds to be very firm about this date, as we had seen several cases of would-be cruisers who delayed their departure time and again, until it was too late. The argument would be, "If I just work one more year . . . I can get x more dollars in my cruising kitty." The next year the argument would be the same. Time would pass, and before long, life would rear its head with some other insurmountable obstacle . . . and that was the end of their cruising dream. We were determined not to let this happen to us. Whatever funds we had available at the end of 2005 . . . would have to be it!

In the meantime, I decided to continue my transformation into a healthy human being by losing weight. Over the years weight had started to pile on. Just a little at first, but once the drinking got heavier, the alcohol had added many unwanted calories to my intake and I found myself . . . well . . . fat.

I used to tell myself that it didn't matter. I had been slim and attractive most of my life. "Been there...done that!" I was still very active, despite my added weight. I was a scuba diver (with a *huge* custom-made wetsuit). I sailed. I went for hikes, climbed mountains. I wasn't a couch potato stuffing cream cakes all day. Nevertheless, I was what some would kindly call heavy or stout. In other words . . . fat! The moment of truth came to me one day when I was trying to retrieve something from a tight spot on the boat. My hips would just not allow me to go into that particular space. I decided then and there . . . No good! Gotta do something about this!

So, I joined Weight Watchers and revised my diet. It took me seven months, but I lost thirty-six kilos, about a third of my body weight. It was really not hard. It was thrilling to watch myself shrink. I guess, having already changed my habits drastically by quitting the booze, it was a natural progression to change what I ate.

It seemed to me that someone had just turned a big switch on my forehead. My whole attitude to life had changed. I had changed.

I suppose the AA meetings helped too. Attending AA meetings is a huge privilege. People imagine a bunch of former drunks sitting around telling horror stories of their drinking days. That's what I thought too, the first time I reluctantly attended one, on the advice of my counsellors. That's not it at all. I was shocked at the calibre of the people at AA. In general, the people there were bright, good-looking, often successful people who had all, at some stage in their life, had a serious problem. They came from all walks of life, but had a lot of character traits in common. To varying degrees, we were all control freaks and emotional with it, with a skewed view of life and our place in it. AA meetings were all about sharing with one another, our day-to-day battle with our own skewed view of things and how to change this.

In any case, by the end of that first sober year, I was slimmer and healthier than I had ever been. Or so I thought. As it turns out, I might have unknowingly helped to save my life by changing my eating habits during that particular year. Because I was about to be shat upon from a great height.

For about a year I had had a freckle on the tip of my nose. I had it removed by my doctor who told me it was nothing to worry about. But . . . it came back. In the end I was sent to a specialist who immediately suspected trouble. He took an emergency biopsy. The very next day, I got the phone call that I was dreading. The "freckle" was a melanoma, and a bad one. It had already penetrated the skin, probably releasing little cancer "seeds" into my lymphatic system and perhaps even my bloodstream. I was told that I would have to have my nose removed and that statistically my chances of surviving the next ten years were down to sixty percent.

I had heard of melanoma, but knew lots of people who had skin cancer and just had bits removed and carried on their lives. Now I learned that there are many types of skin cancer but only one that will kill you, melanoma. It is often terminal because it penetrates into the body and creates secondary cancers in the liver, lungs, or brain.

I was stunned! All my dreams of sailing, of sun-drenched beaches and crystal water, were crashing down around my ears. Forget sailing off into the sunset. I would be lucky to survive! I called Chris and we went to lunch at a restaurant with a terrace looking out over the sea. We just sat there quietly and cried.

It was hard to think. Hard to believe it was real. In the last few years, we had lost no fewer than three friends to cancer, all of them within three months of diagnosis. It was very, very scary.

After awhile, Chris said, "I'd better cancel that presentation we were going to have on the boat this evening."

I had forgotten about that. We had scheduled a meeting that

evening to introduce a young woman to our direct sales business. She was a really nice person and seemed very interested in what we had to say. We hoped that she might join our business. Every little bit helped. This was all part of working toward our dream. However, now we both wondered, Is there any point now? Have our priorities changed? Are we still working toward our ten year goal, now only a couple of years away?

I made a decision then and there, and it was a decision that got me through the next couple of years. I was *not* going to give up on anything! I would fight this thing and I *would* go sailing. We would *not* cancel the meeting. We would present our business and we would do it well.

The presentation that evening on our boat took three hours. I don't think I was ever before so passionate about introducing someone to our business. And for those three hours, I did not even think about cancer.

The young woman decided to join our business and I had my answer on how to proceed with my life. I would do what was required for my health, but it would be a side issue in my life. I would continue on as before and work on the assumption that I would still be around to sail the world. If anything, I planned to work even harder to make this dream happen.

Six surgeries followed, as well as a trip to Australia for a special scan that could not be performed in New Zealand at the time. I lost my nose to the cancer, and got a new one made from the skin on my forehead. A "forehead-flap reconstruction," it was called. The surgeons did an amazing job, and although I looked different, I was not horrific to look at.

Chris joked that "Not everyone has a chance to have two noses in one lifetime."

Throughout, I continued to view the cancer and surgeries as a side issue. I remember coming out of the first nose surgery. I looked appalling. There was a railroad track of black stitches vertically across my forehead. Under the bandage across my nose, there was an open wound, where they had attached the new skin in a flap, which was to become the new nose. The forehead flap had to stay attached both to the nose and the forehead until a blood-supply was established to the new nose. This would take a few weeks. I looked like something out of a monster story.

But . . . there was a really interesting seminar relating to our business that was scheduled for the very next day, in Auckland, five hundred kilometres away. I decided to attend.

The doctors took some convincing to even let me out of the

hospital, let alone permit Chris to drive me five hundred kilometres across New Zealand to attend a seminar. But . . . attend . . . I did.

Years later, people still remembered what I looked like that day. Apparently, people found it inspirational to see me there. It was not my intention to inspire anyone. I was just selfishly trying to stay one step ahead of the abyss.

Nevertheless, one person told me, years later, "Every time I feel too lazy to get off my couch to attend a seminar or a meeting, I think of you there, with your bandaged face. And I think, if she could be there *like that*, then I can sure as hell get off this couch and get myself down there!"

After the initial nose-replacement there followed a couple of surgeries to remove lymph nodes from my neck.

After one of these I was lame around the mouth and had a crooked smile and dribbled my food for a year. Charming! Life was definitely teaching me some lessons about letting go of my vanity!

Still, I continued to take the surgeries in my stride and absolutely refused to let them get me down. On one occasion, I was still attached to a pump, after a lymph node surgery performed the previous day. We had been invited to the horse races.

"Let's go!" I hid all the tubes under some scarves and off we went.

Two days after the second lymph node surgery, I participated in a mini-triathlon. Because . . . I had signed up for it months ago! I was hell-bent on not letting this *thing* interfere with my life.

It was interesting too, that I never felt the need to reach for my "crutch," alcohol, during this time. Initially, I did think it was a little unfair that this should happen to me now.

I remember thinking After all, I have gone to great lengths to change my life. I have kicked my alcohol habit. I have lost the weight. I have turned myself around. Is this my reward!?

I thought back to a time, when I was newly sober . . . and still a little angry about having to give up booze. I had attended an AA meeting where they spoke about an AA member that had just died of cancer. They were all so happy for her and proud of her, because she had died sober.

I remember thinking What a fool! If I was told that I was dying of cancer, I would go for it, all stops out . . . eat and drink whatever you like . . . Enjoy it while you can!

Strangely enough, a year down the track, when it did happen to me, the absolutely last thing I wanted to do was reach for a drink.

It was then that it dawned on me how much my thinking had changed. A year previously I had felt sorry for myself to have to change my life and give up alcohol. Drinking still felt like a privilege that I was being denied. Poor me!

Now I had grown to understand that life without booze . . . a life with complete clarity, remembering everything about my day, every day . . . was the privilege. The very last thing I wanted . . . if I was to have limited time on this earth . . . was to waste that time in a drunken haze.

Anyway, things got better. There were no signs of the cancer having spread. However, I was warned not to get too hopeful. Melanoma is one of the most aggressive of all the various cancers. Unfortunately it does not respond to the traditional treatments either. So radiotherapy and chemo don't help. In one way this is a good thing, because it saves you from having to endure these horrible treatments. In another way, it leaves you with no weapons against the disease. You just have to hope that if it does spread, it will be detected early and that the bit affected can be removed.

Again, I was humbled by all the support I got. Both friends and complete strangers showed me so much kindness. It was overwhelming.

I remember walking through a mall one day, a bandage still on my nose. A lady, a complete stranger, came up to me and said "What is your name, dear?" I told her, and she said, "I will pray for you!"

Many, many people suggested various treatments that would help. They all meant well, even though some of the suggestions bordered on the bizarre. In the end, it started to make me feel uncomfortable. There were so many alternative treatments, so many "magic remedies" offered, that it was impossible to try them all. I had to choose, and if I chose wrong, it felt like it would be my own fault if I died.

I decided to be rational about it and listen carefully to everyone, before I made a choice. I would listen and see if something kept coming up. Where there is smoke, there is fire, I thought. Perhaps there is some truth to it, if I am told about a cure from many different sources.

Apricot kernels kept coming up. They were called the "homeopathic chemotherapy." They contain a type of cyanide that is reputed to attack cancer cells while leaving the good guys intact. Too many would poison you, but in a controlled dose taken daily, they might help.

I decided to give it a go. I also decided to work really hard at keeping my immune system in good trim. The healthy diet I was already on since losing the weight now got even healthier. Finally, I decided that I needed as much positive mental energy in my life as possible. I read uplifting books, watched funny movies, hung around with upbeat people, stayed away from hospitals as much as possible, and even stopped reading newspapers and watching news programmes. To my mind that was all gloom and doom . . . If something important happens I will find out one way or another, I told myself.

Slowly I started to feel like I was managing to shake off the sticky spider web of disease that I felt was trying to imprison me. I was more determined than ever to get on a boat and escape off into the sunset.

CHAPTER 5

December of 2005 arrived. This was the month which we had long ago promised ourselves would be the last month that we would work; this was our retirement deadline. Because of all the health issues, I was already only working part-time.

But, for Chris, this was a very big change. I think a lot of his co-workers were as excited as he was about his leaving. The dream-stealers had been quiet for awhile, and those who were inspired by our dogged and persistent progress toward our goal were delighted for us. There was a wonderful and emotional retirement party, with banners of *"Bon Voyage"* flying for all to see. His co-workers had even recorded a DVD for him, which ended with an image of the Mana harbour exit, our gateway to the beginning of the adventure. It felt fantastic.

We left in the new year, to make our way up to the north of New Zealand. The plan was to spend the next year in Opua, in the Bay of Islands, and make our final preparations there. Opua was where all the international cruisers moored when they came to New Zealand. It was the preferred port of departure when heading off for the Pacific islands. It would be the perfect place to get ready to go and to purchase all the equipment that we still needed, for instance, solar panels, autopilot, life raft, etc., etc. We had already installed a brand new engine, but there was lots of stuff we still needed.

As we still had no autopilot, we again took along crew for the sail north. After a bit of a shaky start with one of our rigging wires snapping due to strong winds, we headed up the West Coast of the North Island. We were a little apprehensive after our rough ride down the East Coast four years earlier, but all went well. We arrived safely in Opua and immediately set to work.

It was a glorious time! I remember that last year in Opua before departure as one of the best years of my life.

As soon as we got there, we were a part of an international cruising fraternity. It was so easy to make friends; it was so easy to talk to these people. In our home port of Mana, we had been the odd ones out . . . the only ones who were planning to set off and sail into the sunset. Here in Opua, we were just one couple among all the rest of the cruisers. We were the rookies among seasoned sailors who had done what we intended to do for many years. We felt an immediate kinship with these people.

We had to pinch ourselves! It is really going to happen! Ten years . . . and we are on the final stretch!

A small aside, now, to those of you who still think that you would like to do this, who still think that we are something special, who still think that you couldn't manage it financially. Remember, it looked impossible to us in the beginning too. We needed a boat, and we needed capital to provide income.

Without going into too much financial detail, here is how it came together. We paid off our house and then sold it. The house, nothing special and quite small, provided NZ$225,000. This purchased the boat for $156,000 with a bit of change to go into investments and savings. We put every bit of spare change from our jobs and our business into the stock market. At the time, the markets were in an upswing, so our kitty grew quite a bit over the years. Finally, when we retired, we cashed in our retirement funds and sold the car and the camper van. We had aimed at capital of $150,000 and we did not quite achieve that. But, even after spending about $80,000 buying a new engine, solar panels, autopilot, new VHF, new radio, new rudder, new anchor, chain, lines, life raft, etc., etc., etc., we did end up with about $120,000 in investments. With Chris' small pension from the UK and some rent money, we would achieve a monthly income of around NZ$1,200 – $1,300. This would just have to do. And it did. There were certainly many cruisers out there who were better off than us, but there were others who had an even smaller monthly income. We would have to be careful, but we would not starve.

So, all was going well, all was going according to plan. We were in an almost constant state of euphoria. At the same time, we were working very hard, getting everything ready. We had also promised our family in the UK that we would pay them a final visit that August, as we did not know when we would see them again after we set off into the Pacific.

However, life was not finished testing us yet. The spider web was again reaching out toward me with its sticky threads.

In April, I discovered a lump, under the skin just south of my right cheekbone, first the size of a raisin, then the size of an olive. I ignored it for as long as I could . . . pushed it out of my mind . . . thought that I could make it go away by wishing it so . . . willing it out of existence.

Nope . . . didn't work.

In the end, I had to go back to the doctors. It was secondary melanoma. Those little "seeds" of melanoma had travelled through my system and metastasised. They settled in my parotid gland.

So . . . more surgery. I returned to Wellington, to my doctors there, this time staying with a friend who kindly took us in as we had nowhere to stay.

After the surgery to remove the parotid gland, there were more scans and they seemed to indicate further spread to other lymph nodes. Another surgery followed.

After this one I partially lost the use of my right arm. The nerves had been exposed in the surgery and it was uncertain whether I would regain full movement. I worried that this would impair my abilities to handle sails, etc.

In general the news was grim. Primary cancer can still be cured, if you are lucky. Secondary cancer is not usually curable. It becomes a matter of "When" not "If." I was told that I now had only a twenty-five percent chance of surviving the next five years. Despite there not being a shred of evidence that it helps with melanoma, they wanted me to have radiation therapy. I would probably lose my taste buds and salivary glands, not to mention ongoing dental problems and burns to my face. I decided to decline.

I must admit that this was a low point. It was hard to stay buoyant. I had to stop and rethink things. It seemed that my time was destined to be limited. I would probably get ill again sometime in the near future. Where we were planning to go, there would be no decent hospitals, and there might be many miles between doctors. I was advised that I would need to be "seen" every three months.

On the other hand, my whole being was infused with the need to *go . . . get out . . . Go!*

It was not even any more just a wish. It felt like a necessity.

In my heart, I knew for certain, that if I did the "wise" thing and stayed, cancelled the trip of my dreams . . . I would die. I would be waiting to die. Every time I was in a hospital or sat in front of a doctor, I could hear their unspoken message . . . So sorry, but you may as well face it . . . Your chances are slim.

Don't get me wrong. These were fantastic doctors and I will always be incredibly grateful to them for all that they did. The plastic surgeon who made me a new nose did such a good job that it looks like I was born with it. They were all wonderful. But . . . they had their statistics, and in their experience I was probably not going to make it.

In the end, the decision was not difficult at all for me. If my time was limited, I knew how I wanted to spend it. If I only got to sail one stretch, if I only got to visit one island, if I only got to walk on one beach . . . it would be worth years of any "extra time" that I might have by being "sensible." I told my specialist that I would take responsibility for my own wellbeing and left.

We went to the UK in August. I spent the whole month there following a physical training program of my own invention, involving exercises and swimming, to try to regain full use of my right arm. It was pretty much successful. The arm is clumsier than it was, and not as strong . . . but it serves me well.

We returned to the boat, in Opua, put the last cancer episode out of our minds, and continued with preparations. I was again exactly where I wanted to be and loving it! The departure from New Zealand got ever closer.

CHAPTER 6

The day had finally arrived! After ten years of planning, working, dreaming, and focus, we were set to leave the shores of our adopted country, New Zealand. We had lived here for the last fifteen years, becoming citizens along the way. Though Chris is a native of the UK and I was born a Swede, we sailed on our New Zealand passports, and *Skylark II* was a New Zealand registered vessel. This country had been incredibly kind to us. We had enjoyed our time here. It is a gentle country with nature as beautiful as any you will ever see anywhere. But the sundrenched shores of the Pacific beckoned.

For our first offshore leg, we had decided to sail in company with other boats, so we joined the Island Cruising Association's annual "New Zealand to Tonga Rally." The stretch of ocean between New Zealand and the southernmost of the Pacific Islands is notorious for bad blows, and we were therefore a little wary. We knew that joining a rally would mean that we would get the very best weather information. We would also be on a daily roll call in case of trouble. Besides, we had heard it was fun . . . like a casual race . . . with lots of silly activities once we reached Tonga.

The day of departure was set for May 7th, 2007. All rally skippers met daily to check out the weather forecasts. We were also getting advice from New Zealand's number one weather guru. The problem with setting a firm departure date, of course, is that it is counterintuitive to sailing wisdom, which says choose your day of departure based on weather, not on the calendar. Obviously it was up to each individual skipper to decide if they would leave on the given date . . . but . . . you know . . . it's like in high school . . . there is a lot of peer pressure.

As the day approached, it did not look that good to us. There was a wee blip in the weather picture a few days out. It might develop into something. The debate ran hot among the skippers, but in the end, the majority decided it was a *"Go."* Not wanting to be the only wimps that bowed out, we buried our misgivings and prepared for departure.

It was a glorious day! One that will be forever indelibly etched into our memory. All the rally boats, about twenty of us, in a long line, sailed past the Opua Yacht Club terrace, where family and friends had gathered to see us off. For most of the boats in the rally, this was a six month affair and they would be back in New Zealand at the end of the season. But that was not our agenda.

This was it! We were leaving, really leaving . . . sailing off into the sunset to adventures unknown.

We had done it! We had actually done it!

And then the main halyard winch broke! Literally as we were sailing past the yacht club!

Knowing that there would be no chandleries in Tonga to provide boat supplies and equipment . . . Chris said "We have to turn back!"

I just could not bear it. I was so desperate to get out of the clutches of that sticky spider web, which I felt had done its best to hold me back, to stop me from leaving. I just could not contemplate it. I could *not* turn back. I think Chris understood.

Though he is an extremely cautious sailor, he said, "I guess I can make a temporary fix. It will be okay."

And with that, the last sticky thread let go of us . . . and we were away.

The first couple of days went well. When long distance sailing, your life revolves around the clock. You are aware of the time all through the day and night, because the clock decides when you are on watch and when you can relax. Chris and I do three hour shifts in the night and four hour shifts in daytime. Everything revolves around that.

Non-sailors sometimes have this romantic picture of the sailing couple clinking glasses in the cockpit as they watch the sun set over the unending horizon. Perhaps, once in a blue moon . . . but the reality is usually different. At least for the first few days you are tired all the time, so when you are not on watch you head straight for your bunk for a few hours of sleep. You hardly see one another except for the change of watch.

Being on watch also means being in command. When it is rough, or cold, it means being out in the exposed cockpit while your partner is cosy, warm, and dry below. Often you are counting the minutes until you can pass over responsibility and head below. If you see the dark clouds of a squall approaching, you pray that it will hold off until you can hand over! Sounds mean? Okay, fellow cruisers, come on . . . don't tell me you have never thought like that! I am just being honest here!

There are nights though, when it is heaven being out there in the cockpit alone at night. You have never seen stars like you see them at sea. There are no land lights to obscure the view, and the sky goes on forever. Never seen a shooting star? Just spend ten minutes at night, at sea, gazing above you . . . and I pretty much guarantee you will see one.

And how wonderful . . . how incredible . . . that you are looking at something that all those ancient seafarers before you also saw. Captain James Cook . . . having just discovered New Zealand, was looking at that same sky. Before him, the Maori approaching the Land of the Long White Cloud . . . shared this view with you.

And then there is the dawn! How often, when living on land, do you get up to watch the break of dawn? Unless you are very unusual, or perhaps at a teenage all night party, it rarely happens . . . Am I right?

When at sea, glorious sunsets and sunrises are a daily treat. Lots of people before me have waxed lyrical about how you "become one with nature" on a small boat in a vast ocean. They are right. You can't help it. Your very existence is ruled by the rhythms of day and night, of calm or storm, of rain or sunshine. You are exposed to the elements in a way that you never are on land, not even in a tent on a stormy night. You can prepare all you like. You can have the safest, most comfortable boat that money can buy. You can equip it with the latest technology. You can study all the courses. In the end, you point that boat in the direction you want to go, you set your sails . . . and then it is down to nature. You cannot control whether you will have a bumpy ride or a smooth one, whether you will be wet, cold, and miserable . . . or sipping cocktails in the cockpit. Once you are at sea, you just do the best you can with what is sent in your direction.

Like life really! In a condensed version.

A few days out, life decided to send us a rough patch. The little blip we had seen in the weather developed into what is sometimes called "an eggbeater phenomenon." This is when two circular weather formations are trying to jostle for space and you get stuck in the middle between them. Unlike ordinary storms, which will usually be fairly short-lived as the weather moves on, in an eggbeater the weather systems can't go anywhere. This means high winds and waves day after day after day.

In the scheme of things, our eggbeater was not a very severe one. We had winds of around thirty-five to forty knots and five to six meter waves.

But it just seemed to go on forever. Chris and I got more and more tired. We were battling the elements when on watch, but also could not sleep well as the boat was being buffeted by the huge seas. By day four, we felt ourselves getting to the stage where we were not thinking clearly any more. We had heard, over the roll call, that a couple of the boats had sustained damage; one almost sank when a hatch broke and flooded their forward compartment.

A couple of other boats had decided to deploy their parachute anchors and wait it out. We decided to do the same.

Again, we were amazed at how well this strategy worked. I can't say that we were comfortable on sea anchor . . . You are still thrown around a lot. The best way I can describe it is that it feels like being inside a pinball machine, and you are the ball. If you don't hang on tight to something at all times, you tend to get thrown into the furniture. But, still, things are calm enough to make a hot meal, to get some sleep, to calm down and gather your thoughts.

By dawn the next day we were ready to go again.

Not a chance! The waves were way too high to risk the manoeuvre of trying to retrieve the parachute. We would have to wait until things calmed down a bit. All the while, those boats that had opted to continue were getting closer to paradise without us. Frustrating! It took forty-eight hours on parachute anchor before we were able to continue.

The passage between Opua and Tonga is about a thousand sea miles. We sail at an average of five knots (nautical miles per hour), actually a little faster, but we conservatively calculate with five knots. That means that we can usually cover 120 miles in a twenty-four hour period. Thus, the passage to Tonga in a straight line would be about eight days. However we would not be going in a straight line, we would be beating, so we could expect about ten days out of sight of land.

For those of you who find ten days at sea pretty scary . . . Well, we do too. It is a long stretch even for blue water cruisers. Except for crossing the Atlantic, or the northern Pacific, this is one of the longest runs. In fact, in the six years of cruising that we now have behind us, this was our longest crossing. A lot of the world can be seen with day-hops or possibly one overnighter. In the Pacific, you sometimes do two or three day passages, but rarely more than a week.

This passage was also the toughest from a weather perspective. So far, it seemed that we were encountering our share of heavy blows. However, we were not too discouraged by this. We knew that things would get better, the further north we got. The waters surrounding New Zealand do have a fearsome reputation for nasty weather. We reckoned that the worst we would see would be up front. Once through that gauntlet, weather conditions would improve. This did prove to be the case.

On this long passage, given the right conditions, there was a chance for a break. Smack dab in the middle of nowhere, about

250 miles southwest of Tonga, there are two mid-ocean reefs called South Minerva Reef and North Minerva Reef. Just a few decades ago, before the advent of precise navigation tools like GPS, these were areas that you avoided at all cost. They were a hazard to navigation and you made sure you stayed well clear. Not so today. GPS is now so accurate that you can not only avoid these reefs easily, but if you wish, you can take shelter within them. They are large, and although completely submerged at high tide, they have a shallow sand lagoon at their centre. If you can find the reef entrance and have the courage to sail through it, a haven awaits you within. We were determined to try.

We headed for North Minerva Reef, and despite having read about the place, we were still pretty surprised and not a little awestruck when we got there. Imagine sailing for a week or more with nothing but blue ocean around you. You get used to that view, used to the sound of the boat and the waves. All of a sudden there is a roar in the distance, and soon a white line breaks the blue of your horizon. It is loud and the breakers are big. We approached cautiously and sailed along the reef, keeping a good distance from the breakers. We sailed right past where our GPS said that the reef entrance was, but could see nothing. It looked like an unbroken line of breaking waves.

We sailed back past it again. Still nothing to see.

Was the GPS wrong? We were too chicken to go closer.

We were torn. It would be so wonderful to put an anchor down, go for a swim . . . sleep for eight hours straight. The alternative was to carry on to Tonga, another two or three days away.

Oh please! Where is that entrance?

Then we remembered that we had heard on the radio that some friends of ours were not too far distant. We had met Fatty and Carolyn Goodlander, an American couple, in Opua. They had invited us to dinner on their yacht, *Wild Card*, before our departure. Although they were not part of the rally, they had left New Zealand at about the same time as us and had also resorted to their parachute anchor in the storm. We believed they were planning a stop at North Minerva.

We tried them on the VHF. Sure enough, Fatty replied and told us that he was, indeed, headed for North Minerva, in fact would be arriving there in about a half hour. We told him that we were feeling very uncertain about making the reef entrance, this being our very first one. We asked if we could follow him in.

Initially, I think, he was pretty reluctant, understandably so. After all, we needed to stand on our own two feet . . . or keel, as it were.

The concern was that if we followed him through the narrow passage and got too close, we would be crowding his space and making any manoeuvres on his part more difficult, possibly endangering his boat.

He tried to discourage us from waiting by giving us a bit of a pep talk on the radio. "You can do it!" "We are still a half hour away; you don't want to wait!"

But . . . we stuck to him like glue and he could not shake us off. Being a thoroughly good guy, in the end he relented and set some basic rules. We were to keep a good distance in case he had to turn back and be sure to get out of his way.

Following *Wild Card*, we "shot the pass" without problems, though it did make our hearts beat faster as we made our way through the huge breakers.

Later, Fatty, who is an author, wrote an article in *Cruising World Magazine* called "Shooting the Pass" about this incident, using the story as a platform to teach other sailors how to make an approach to a reef entrance safely.

Being in the lagoon was heaven! We anchored next to *Wild Card* in crystal clear, impossibly blue water over a fine sand bottom. We invited them over for a drink and nibbles on *Skylark* and watched in awe as the tide came in and completely covered the reef. It was really bizarre! No land in sight anywhere, just Pacific Ocean as far as the eye could see. And yet, we were safely anchored in calm water. We slept very, very well that night.

We spent the next couple of days swimming, relaxing, and socialising with Fatty and Carolyn. They are an amazing couple and we were destined to become firm friends, even though we rarely spent more than a few days with them in the same anchorage. But we were roughly following the same path and were to meet up with them many times.

One of the incredible bonuses that the cruising life brings is the people you have the privilege of meeting. I don't know of any other activity in life that gets you together with so many interesting and inspirational people.

I know, I know . . . there are plenty of wonderful people on land too . . . but among the cruisers, it seems that everyone just has that extra bit of quirkiness. I suppose we are all just a little nuts. You have to be, to push your boundaries beyond that safety net of land-living.

And, among this group of quirky cruisers, there are just some that you know you will never forget. For us, Fatty and Carolyn come into that category.

Fatty has pretty much always been a live-aboard. Not many can say that! When he was very young, his Dad, whom he describes as an "anarchist and an artist" moved his whole family aboard a yacht. This was in the days when it was still not very common to do so. Fatty got his schooling here and there and was often targeted by the "do-gooders," the ladies in sensible shoes, who used to come down to their boat to implore his parents to put him in a proper school. He remembers looking out of the porthole and seeing those sensible shoes and running and hiding in some invisible nook on the boat.

Despite this sketchy education, Fatty has become an author and supports himself, his wife, and his cruising by writing articles and stories about his cruising adventures. I really love his autobiographical book *Chasing the Horizon*. He describes, better than anyone I know, why it is that we cruisers do what we do. What it is that drives us.

But my favourite story is how their boat got its name, *Wild Card*.

At the time, Fatty and Carolyn and their eight year old daughter, Roma Orion, were living on a concrete boat which they had built themselves, in the Virgin Islands. They had invested everything they owned into this boat. It was more than a cruising boat; it was their home, all that they had.

A strong hurricane was forecast, Hurricane Hugo, but they had some warning, and so they had positioned themselves in a relatively safe spot off the island of Culebra near some mangroves and set anchors all around. As the winds picked up and it got very noisy, their young daughter got frightened by the noise. Fatty told her not to worry. All would be well. Apparently, she had her own little cabin on their boat.

Even though their boat was well secured, a boat nearby broke its moorings and started to bear down on them. Fatty realised that there was nothing they could do, they would be hit by this boat, and that is what happened. In the collision, a stanchion was driven right through the deck into the little girl's cabin. Fortunately nobody was hurt.

However, Roma asked her Dad, "Can I be worried now?"

Fatty and Carolyn realised that they would lose their boat. The damage caused by the other boat was too severe. They decided to try to make it to land.

So, they attached Roma's passport to her belly with duct tape (just in case), put warm clothes on her, and a life-vest with a rope attached to it. The plan was for Fatty to take the girl and try to swim to shore. Carolyn would remain on the boat and was instructed to pull like hell if something happened to Fatty, or they got stuck. At least she would hopefully get her daughter back. Carolyn describes this as one of the scariest moments of her life.

Fortunately, Fatty made it to shore with Roma, and Carolyn then followed.

Now they were in some remote place, in the middle of a hurricane, wet and without shelter. But . . . they saw an empty holiday home in the distance. They made for that.

Apparently Roma has never forgotten the moment when her mother, pumped full of adrenaline and a powerful maternal instinct, kicked the door in . . . no trouble.

In the hours and days that followed, they were joined by other bedraggled survivors of the hurricane.

Once the excitement of their rescue had died down, reality and depression set in. They had lost everything. Fatty was faced with a situation where he had a wife and young daughter to support and nothing, no home, no money, nothing. It got him really down at first, but then he knew he would have to pull his socks up.

By now they were back on the main island of St. John and were "couch surfing" with friends.

Fatty took a tour of the devastated island and looked at all the boats, even the ones that had sunk.

Then he received a phone call from a friend of his who told him that he too had lost his boat. She was a thirty-eight foot Sparkman and Stevens sloop and was still sitting on a reef with a big hole in her.

Fatty went and had a look at her. She was in pretty bad shape, but he thought he might be able to fix her up.

Next he made the rounds to all his friends and family, pleading for a small loan, whatever they could spare.

With $50 here and $100 there, he managed to be able to scrape together $3000. He pleaded with his friend to be able to buy the boat...as is...on the reef...for $3000. The friend, disillusioned with boats and hurricanes, agreed.

In the months that followed, Fatty salvaged the boat and patched her up.

One day, Carolyn came along with Roma, to watch progress.

"We were playing life's game just fine . . . We had all our cards in order . . . and then, Wham! along comes Hugo," she said. "Hugo is a wild card tossed into our lives at 180 miles per hour."

Thus the name of their boat became *Wild Card.* When we met

them, Fatty and Carolyn were on their second circumnavigation in *Wild Card*.

Soon though, even the companionship of Fatty and Carolyn could not dampen the excitement of the upcoming landfall in Tonga. We up-anchored, left the calm of the reef, and continued on our way.

CHAPTER 7

We left Minerva Reef after a couple of days of glorious R&R, and headed out into the Pacific for the remaining 250 miles to Tonga. This part of the trip was uneventful. The bad weather had passed and we were sailing along in a crisp, warm breeze. It was as sailing should be. The cold weather clothing was off, the shorts and T-shirts were on. Sun cream was required. It was absolutely glorious!

It's funny, you know. Seafaring stories, books about maritime adventures, articles about sailing . . . even this one . . . are all about the times when things go wrong. When I think about the books I have read, they are all about survival at sea after a sinking, about how someone lost someone overboard, how to survive a hurricane, etc., etc. We all seem to thrive on the dramatic.

The truth is that, in my experience, bad weather and disasters are the exception, not the norm of the cruising life. For ninety to ninety-five percent of the time, life is gravy, winds are light, and the sun is shining. The pace of life on board goes from the desperate to the sublime. Though you are still ruled by the clock and your watches, you do more with your day than just grimly hang in there. People often ask about this . . . "Are you not bored out there? What is there to do on a small boat in the middle of an ocean for days on end?" Others may experience it differently, but speaking for myself, I am never bored at sea. There seems to be lots to do all the time.

A typical day then . . . how does it look?

Let's say that Chris had the dawn watch and woke me up at 6 a.m. It is light outside . . . How nice! I sit and enjoy my cup of coffee in the cockpit. I think about last night and my two night watches, now behind me. I calculate which day of our present leg we are on. How many more days to go? Wow, only two more days! In forty-eight hours or so, we will be there. Amazing! *Beep! Beep!* Oh . . . the watch alarm. Fifteen minutes have passed.

Chris and I have a watch alarm. It is a kind of sophisticated, custom-built egg timer, which you can set to go off at any time interval you want. We have ours set at fifteen minutes, as this is usually the time it might take for a modern freight ship to travel from our first sighting of it to our location. Thus, we want to make sure that we scan the horizon carefully, every fifteen minutes, to see if anything is out there. Once the timer beeps, you must press a button on it and it resets itself. The beep is initially quiet, so as not to wake up your sleeping partner. However, if you don't press the button, it gets angrier and angrier, with the beeps getting louder and more frequent and lights blinking red. If you continue to not press the button, perhaps because you are disabled or have fallen overboard, a very loud . . . piercingly loud . . . alarm goes off in the cabin below to alert your partner that all is not well on deck.

So, the watch alarm has gone off and I scan the horizon. No one out there. Great!

I cast a quick glance at the laptop, which is below and running a navigation program. The screen shows an image of a red boat, following a yellow route, which Chris has pre-programmed before departure. As we follow the route, it turns red behind our virtual boat. I check that we are not deviating too much from the intended route and make adjustments on the autopilot as needed. I also check a display that gives our speed, time to go, and distance to go. By the time I have finished fiddling with all this, the watch alarm beeps again. I climb back into the cockpit for another look around.

All is well. Time to make myself another coffee and some fruit salad for breakfast.

Everything is done in fifteen minute intervals, well, ten minute intervals really, because it probably takes five minutes to check the horizon carefully each time. By the time I have made and eaten breakfast, and quietly cleared up the dishes, an hour and a half have probably passed. I settle down for a good read, for the next hour or so.

Our daytime watches are four hours on, four hours off, to give the off-watch partner a bit more time in one stretch, for a decent sleep. Even so, you very quickly fall into the routine of only sleeping three hours at a time. By about 9 a.m., Chris wakes up and I make him a cup of tea. We spend the next hour catching up, chatting, discussing how long until landfall, talking about what special tasks we might attempt today.

At 10 a.m., I hand over the watch to Chris and go below for a little shut-eye.

A couple of hours later, Chris wakes me up for lunch. Even at sea, we try to have a salad. When we run out of lettuce, there is always cabbage turned into coleslaw. We also grow our own sprouts. I have a three-tier sprouting jar which dangles amidships near the galley and provides a steady supply of "crunch" for our salads. We also make our own yoghurt and bread on board, all activities that take up part of our day.

After lunch, I wash up and prepare the dough for the next loaf of bread. I decide on what we will have for the evening meal . . .

just potter really.

Before long, Chris announces that it is 2 p.m. and time for me to take over. He goes below for a nap. I take my cup of coffee into the cockpit. *Beep! Beep!* Time to look around. I settle down for another couple of hours of reading.

It is 4 p.m. and time for roll call. On the New Zealand to Tonga trip, there was a daily roll call, organised by the rally. However, with or without a formal rally, Chris and I usually join a ham net roll call for safety. We are both ham radio licensed and have found this to be a great advantage. In most locations in the world there are "nets" set up by volunteers on land, which track small boats at sea. On departure you join a net and are put on their "roll." This means that they will be calling you up on a certain frequency at a certain time of day. You must report where you are, what the sea and weather conditions are, and whether all is well on board. The net usually provides a weather forecast for your area. They also worry about you if you fail to report in, and take appropriate action, should you go missing for long.

Because our ham radio interferes with our autopilot, answering the roll call is a two man activity on our boat. One of us has to hand-steer the boat, while the other is below on the radio. We tune in and listen to the weather. We also listen to all the other boats and what they are reporting for the weather in their area. This is useful, because it will give us a clue as to what is happening with the weather ahead of or behind us. The roll call typically takes up to an hour. We also take the opportunity to check our emails and possibly send some. Again, through a network of volunteer ham stations, we can send and receive an hour's worth of free email through the ham radio daily. This is brilliant, as it enables us to keep family informed that all is well, and also enables us to receive weather information by email.

By the time all this flurry of activity is over, it is "Happy Hour." Without fail, 5 p.m. is "Happy Hour" on *Skylark*. Chris has a drink and I sip my Diet Coke and we usually have some nibbles. Again, it is one of the rare times of the day when we have time together at sea.

Soon it is time to think about dinner. We try to eat together at 6 p.m., just as the first watch of the night starts. Today, Chris has the first night watch, the sunset watch, 6–9 p.m. We have our dinner and I go below to clear up. One final hot drink and I head for my bunk to sleep for a couple of hours, in anticipation of my first night watch.

Chris wakes me up at 9 p.m. All is well. No ships on the

horizon. He is sleepy and heads straight to bed, knowing that he will be up again at midnight.

I have coffee in the cockpit and try to shake off my sleepiness.

Beep! Beep! Watch alarm. I check the horizon. This time, there is a light, just visible, far away. I get out the binoculars for a closer look. Okay, I can see a red light down low and a white light higher up. Probably a ship passing ahead of us from right to left across our bows. I sit and watch for the next hour as it slowly makes its way past us. This time it was nowhere close. Still, if there is a light out there, I stop all other activity and just watch, until I am a hundred percent sure that it does not pose a threat to us.

Collision is the greatest danger of all, to a cruising yacht. We can survive a storm, but we cannot survive getting run over by a ship.

The rest of my watch passes without incident. I read; I listen to music on the iPod; I press the watch alarm button every fifteen minutes. Midnight comes before I know it. Thank goodness, because I am really getting sleepy now. Can't wait to put my head down! I hand over the watch to Chris and by 12:15 a.m., I hit the pillow.

Oooops! Feels like I barely got to sleep when Chris is there shaking me awake.

It is 3 a.m. and I have the dawn watch. It takes me a good half hour and two cups of coffee to really wake up. I feel woolly in the head. I wish I were still below! Never mind . . . 6 a.m. will be here soon enough. I read my book. My eyes want to close.

Beep! Time to look around! To stay awake I dance about a bit . . . do some stretches. That will get the blood flowing!

Beep! I try to read a little. Boy, am I getting sleepy!

Beep! Time to look around. I dance a little more. I think . . . a snack might help. Piece of salami. Bad for you! Bad girl!! But it helps to wake me up a bit.

Beep! Hello, it is starting to get light. I sit in the cockpit and watch the incredible spectacle of the birth of a new day. No one can ever capture this on film or on canvas. No one could possible reproduce this . . . the real thing . . . the break of dawn. Even if I have seen it hundreds of times by now, it still leaves me with a sense of awe. I am one with nature. Brilliant!

It is now light, and my sleepiness vanishes miraculously. I can see to read without a torch and savour my last hour of the dawn watch. Soon it is 6 a.m. and another twenty-four hours at sea are behind me.

CHAPTER 8

And so, we continued northward.

We were getting really excited now. This would be the very first landfall after leaving New Zealand, the start of our Pacific adventure! Years of longing for a tropical island, a white, sandy beach . . . were about to become reality.

It's funny how we always have this image in our mind of how it will be. For ten years, I had been staring at that Microsoft screensaver of the little tropical island surrounded by impossibly blue water. You know the one! I had invested a lot of emotion into that small tropical island. Sitting under the fluorescent lights of my accounting office, it was my beacon of hope, of better things to come. By preference, I think I would have liked to have found out exactly where that was and headed straight for it. I'm still not quite sure where it is though. There are some who say it is in the Pacific somewhere. Others say it is in the Caribbean or the Maldives.

In any case, reality was that we had to follow a practical and logical route into paradise, and coming from New Zealand, first landfall is usually Tonga, Fiji, or Vanuatu. We had chosen Tonga because it was the farthest east. The prevailing winds in this part of the Pacific blow east to west, so if you go as far east as you can, the sailing to the other islands should be easier.

The New Zealand to Tonga Rally organisers knew that we had all been dreaming of that Microsoft Island, and having been to Tonga before, wanted to make our first landfall special. They couldn't magic up that particular island, but they did want to spare us the disappointment of arriving at the dusty, dirty, busy little main port of the southernmost island Tonga Tapu. This was, however, where cruising boats have to clear into Tonga, that is, go through Customs and Immigration procedures. So, the organisers did the next best thing and negotiated an arrival at an outlying island, not far from Tonga Tapu. They even arranged for the Customs and Immigration officials to come out to the island and clear in the rally boats there.

It wasn't my Microsoft Island; but it was pretty darn good!

There . . . were the palm trees, leaning down over the white sandy beach.

There . . . was the crystal clear tropical blue water.

There . . . was the reef.

There . . . was the scruffy beach bar with a sand floor.

But . . . there . . . was a rusty old hulk decaying in the crystal clear tropical blue water. Oh well, it provided a home for the fish.

I did not know it then, but this was to be the pattern of our experiences, pretty much everywhere. We did find paradise, many of them. (And I'm not moaning. I know how incredibly privileged we have been to experience what we have experienced.) However, just like I firmly believe that every cloud has a silver lining, I equally believe that every silver lining has a teensy cloud. There is always a "but." The trick is to find a positive in every "but." To be happy with what you get, not with what you didn't get. I have come to believe that real happiness lies in enjoying the now, slightly tarnished though it may be. Because it is never quite like you imagined it would be.

In a sense I think this is what drives us, whether on land or at sea. We strive and strive and strive to find perfection, to find that perfect job, that perfect house, that perfect tropical island. In cruising terms, it is what drives you to the next location, "Chasing the horizon," like Fatty says. You are driven to see what comes next. Will the next island be everything that our first landfall was . . . minus the rusting hulk?! Let's go find out!

In any case, we had a great time during the next week. We really enjoyed all the silly Rally Games, such a change from the routine of watches and roll calls. How lovely, to be with people again. How wonderful to make new friends. We were all heading in more or less the same direction and knew that we would meet these people in other anchorages along the way. It was all pretty marvellous. The ten years of preparation melted away, like they had never happened.

Towards the end of the week, our American friend Russ arrived in his tiny boat. He had picked up a young Japanese girl, Taeko, as crew. We had agreed to "buddy boat," sail together, for awhile. Chris and I joked that Russ would be our "training wheels." He knew the area, and we were happy to follow his lead. And so we made our way up the chain of islands that make up Tonga.

Tonga was a wonderful training ground for new cruisers like us. There was so much variety. There are four groups of islands, the southernmost being Tonga Tapu, the capital, where we had made landfall. Here, the modern world intrudes. There is a town, supermarkets, an airport, hotels, restaurants, and bars.

Carrying on northward, you get to the Ha'apai group. These are remote, primitive, low-lying islands, only barely rising out of the surrounding reefs at high tide. There are no harbours. You learn to anchor in between the razor sharp coral formations, taking shelter behind a reef. Shelter means shelter from the waves, not the wind.

The reef will break the waves and leave a calm spot to anchor behind the breakers, but there is no land to break the wind. And it blows!

We were surprised by how much it blew. Most days we had twenty to twenty-five knots. We were also surprised by the water temperature. Sure, you could swim, but it was not the tropical waters I had remembered from the Caribbean. I don't want to imply that we were disappointed. No way! The place was beautiful, exotic, and remote. We were just learning about that "but." There was always a challenge to spice things up. In Tonga in general, it was the wind, and in the Ha'apai Group in particular, the reef anchorages.

When things are going well, you tend to forget that blue water cruising has its fatalities. Sometimes people tell us that they think we are brave, to venture so far from the safety of land. Far from it. We are no heroes. We get as frightened as the next person. We know there are risks. But, we also know that statistically you are far safer at sea than driving on a highway. Statistically you are more likely to die from a bee sting than to be lost at sea.

But it does happen, and on one lovely island in the Ha'apai Group we got an eerie reminder of it.

We had been told that there was the wreck of a trimaran further up the beach and went to investigate. The story was that it had belonged to a young New Zealand couple, who had left their kids in the care of the grandparents and were sailing non-stop from New Zealand to Tahiti. They bumped into one of those eggbeater blows, but a very bad one. When they failed to arrive in Tahiti, Coast Guard planes were sent out to look for them, but to no avail. A few weeks later, parts of their trimaran had washed up on this beach. We went to look for it and there it was! It was a piece from one of the hulls, upside down in the sand. What was so haunting about it was that there was clear evidence that they had survived a while after being capsized. Long enough to scratch "HELP 2 POB" (Help, two persons on board) in the bottom paint of the hull. They had hoped a plane would see it. They were never found.

With that sombre reminder of the dark side of our charmed existence, we continued further north.

On the way, we passed the very spot where the *Mutiny on the Bounty* had happened. This really tickled my fancy! I had read several versions of this true story of Captain Bligh and Fletcher Christian. I guess I was a bit of a *Mutiny on the Bounty* groupie. And there it was. The very spot where the mutineers had forced Captain Bly into a small open boat. There was the volcano-like island where they had tried to get water. This was the view that they had seen from their boat. Wow!

The wows continued in the next island group called Vava'u. Wow!

This was one of the real gems of the South Pacific! It is cruising paradise. The islands lie on a reef plateau, surrounded by an outer reef which disappears into the abyss. The waters inside the outer reef are dotted by small islands, some of them hilly, providing really sheltered bays, and some of them barely peeking over the water's edge . . . Picture the Microsoft Island!

There is a small quaint town, with a few scruffy bars and restaurants and a couple of basic grocery stores. There are a couple of hotels, but not many; it is too remote for any intrusive tourism. There are, however, a couple of bareboat charter outfits, and why wouldn't there be? It really is one of the most fantastic cruising grounds I have ever seen.

Please . . . if you are reading this . . . and are thinking of a bareboat charter . . . go to Vava'u! There are thirty-five perfect and safe anchorages, usually no further apart than a half hour sail. You want to spend the day lazing about on the beach of your very own island? Go to Vava'u. And the bonus . . . drum roll . . . if you are there in June or July . . . you will share the place with huge mummy humpback whales and their young. They travel thousands of miles to this very spot to give birth to, and rear, their young. The waters of Vava'u are warm and shallow, with no predators. It is the perfect whale nursery, and while there, the whales are so mellow, they will often allow you to swim with them.

We really could have stayed there for months . . . years . . . but . . . there is that "but" again, we knew that there was a cyclone season coming up in a couple of months and even the sheltered bays of Vava'u are no match for a cyclone's destructive powers. We needed to continue north and make sure we got to safer waters before the cruising season in the Pacific was over.

Most boats leave Tonga and head for Fiji after Vava'u. However, there is one more Tongan island group, the Niuatoputapu Group, some two hundred miles north of Vava'u. These islands are very remote and not often visited by yachts, and we wanted to check them out.

Indeed, there is not much there other than two small islands and a primitive village. However, the villagers made us very welcome. One enterprising pair had acquired an old VHF radio and welcomed us as we approached the anchorage. They invited us for a meal at their house in the evening. It was a simple affair, served on the floor of their thatched hut. Among the specialties was some kind of roasted small blackbird, which the husband had obviously just captured in the bush. It had bright red feet and legs, and when the bird was put on the fire, this red colour seemed to melt. They used it to make red marks on the cheeks of their small daughter, to her delight.

What stands out in my memories of Niuatoputapu was the strange and tragic incident involving an elderly German man.

When we were at dinner, our hosts said that there was an elderly German living with them. They called him George. We would meet him later, they said, but he had felt unwell, so declined to come to dinner. They indicated that he was asleep in his hut and pointed to a structure that resembled a large dog kennel. It was no more than a metre in height, but long enough for a man to stretch out in. We found this rather odd, but thought no more about it that day.

In the late afternoon of the day following the dinner, our hosts called us on their VHF and asked whether we had seen George. Was he visiting one of the yachts? (There were four of us in the anchorage.) We asked around, but no one had seen him; in fact, none of us had met him at all.

They said that they were a little concerned as George had not showed up for his evening meal. It was his habit to take a walk to the beach on the other side of the island around noon, but he would always be back in the early afternoon. On this day, he had failed to show up. As we had not seen him, they said they would go look for him.

They did not find him that evening and by the morning knew that something was very wrong. They mobilised the whole village to form a search party to scour the island.

We cruisers volunteered to help, but were told, "Thank you, no. This will only confuse the villagers as one foreigner looks the same as another. Better you stay on the boats."

Instead we gathered together all our handheld VHF radios and gave them to the leaders of the search party to ease communications.

It did not take long to find him. The tide was out that morning, and the reef on the other side of the island was exposed. They found George's body in what would have been waist-high water at high tide. He had tied a rope around his waist with a large rock attached to one end.

I remember that the villagers were very confused about this. Suicide is not a part of their culture and they did not know how to react to this.

In any case, they took him back to his native "family" and laid him out according to their traditions. The body was anointed with coconut oil and wrapped in freshly woven palm-leaf mats. They built a small enclosure on the edge of the village, dug a shallow grave in the hard coral ground, and heaped coral rocks over the body. Finally, they put flowers on the grave and someone stuck a cigarette into the rocks because "George liked to smoke."

His native "family" went into mourning, wearing black clothes, which they would wear for a month. They also exhausted their supplies by organising a feast for the whole village, to thank them for having helped in the search.

A few days later, Chris and I went to visit the grave. It was a tragic end to a life, but at the same time I could not help thinking that George had been a lucky guy. None of us knew his story, and neither did his native "family." All they knew is that he had shown up about a year ago. He said he liked the island and would like to stay. He asked for cheap accommodation. He was old and obviously ill. He had eaten with them every day, and slept in the hut they had made him, but kept mostly to himself. He had become a little anxious recently as he was running out of money to pay the small "room and board" required. He must have destroyed or hidden his papers before committing suicide, because they were nowhere to be found. Thus, no one could be notified of his passing.

In my mind, I made up a story about George. I imagined him to be one of these sad and lonely old age pensioners that live isolated in many of our Western cities. How often we have heard of someone being discovered in their flat, weeks after their passing, because they just have no one. It would never happen in other cultures. They look after their old people. They don't stick them in homes or leave them to die alone. There is always someone, some remote family that takes them in. Not so in our "civilised" culture.

Perhaps he had been alone in his flat in Hamburg or Bonn, without family or close relatives, or none he cared about. Perhaps he had a terminal disease. Perhaps he sat there one day in the cold and decided that he wanted to spend his last days in paradise, somewhere warm, somewhere beautiful, somewhere in a place that he had always dreamed of seeing. Perhaps he made his way to this remote Tongan island and decided that this would do nicely. In the end, he was running out of money and felt his disease and his age claiming him. He woke up to another beautiful clear blue sky; another gorgeous Tongan morning. He decided that this would be a good day to die.

That is how I think of him, and yes, George was a lucky man. He was given a caring send-off by his new native family, perhaps a better one than he would have gotten back in Hamburg. He was laid to rest with dignity and ceremony, and his grave would become part of the features on this little corner of paradise.

Rest in peace, George.

CHAPTER 9

After Tonga, we made our way to Fiji, then Tuvalu and then Kiribati. We floated about among the Pacific islands, stopping here and there, sometimes only for a day, sometimes for a week. We saw many, many Microsoft Islands. It was remote, it was beautiful, and it was everything that we had dreamed about. Almost.

Experienced cruisers say that the Pacific islands are the cream of cruising. "Don't rush through! You won't find better anywhere!"

My dreams had us pottering about in this area for months on end, without a care. We would visit places where no one else had been, virgin territory. We would encounter natives that had not seen a foreigner for years, perhaps never!

However, reality is slightly different. Although the more intrepid of the cruisers might deviate and head for uncharted water, practicalities prevent most of us from doing so. It is dangerous out there. Reefs eat boats! You have to be careful. In the end you tend to go to places where others have been before you, just because someone has been there before you. There is information about the reefs and other hazards.

This was the case with us. We were too chicken to deviate much from the beaten track.

Time was also a factor, though we very much did not want it to be. There are seasons for cruising the Pacific. Basically you have between May and November to potter around. Outside of those parameters, you have to find shelter as the cyclone season sets in. You just really, really do not want to be anywhere near a cyclone.

So, there are two options. You either head south to New Zealand or Australia for the off-season (this is what most Pacific cruisers do), or you hightail it way north, past the equator, to the Marshall Islands or thereabouts. We chose the latter option.

And so, we arrived in Kiribati in late October. And then . . . made our way to Abemama and one of the most wonderful experiences in my cruising career.

I will never forget Abemama. I will never forget how a small South Pacific village came together to celebrate the birthday of a stranger . . . me . . . Okay . . . they did love to party . . . and maybe my birthday was just another excuse for a good old *butaki* (party), but still . . . it was a birthday I won't forget.

Abemama is a small, primitive island in the group of small islands and atolls that make up the country of Kiribati. Never heard of Kiribati? . . . Me neither . . . until we got there.

Kiribati lies roughly north of Fiji. There is only one port of entry into the country and that is Tarawa. Coming from Fiji, you actually pass Abemama to get to Tarawa to check in. Then, if you are hell-bent on going to Abemama, you have to retrace your steps in an upwind direction for about seventy-five miles. This puts off most yachts. After all, the country is dotted with tropical paradise islands, so why bother to go through the hassle of sailing upwind to get to this particular one?! You have to have a good reason and we did.

But first, we had to wait a week in Tarawa before the weather eased enough to allow us to attempt it. And a week in Tarawa is a long time.

The less said about Tarawa the better. Some call it the "Armpit of the Pacific," and for good reason. It is overcrowded, dusty, and dirty. On top of that it is eerie. During World War II, thousands of American marines and Japanese soldiers slaughtered each other into oblivion fighting for this tiny insignificant island. "Strategic," apparently. The US marines made a mistake and dropped off their soldiers in waist deep water at high tide. (Got the tide wrong, would you believe it?!) Those poor soldiers had nowhere to go but to wade toward the beach, guns above their heads, only to be mowed down by the Japanese machine guns. There was a horrendous loss of lives. The anchorage is in the very spot where all this happened. It felt like being anchored in a graveyard. Horrible!

Nonetheless we got out of there finally, and headed toward Abemama.

Because it is so inaccessible, Abemama is especially attractive. Not that many yachts stop there. It was one of those off-the-beaten-track places of my dreams. On top of that, we felt we could go there safely, because we were at the time still "buddy boating," that is, sailing together with our American friend Russ. He had been to Abemama before and loved it. Russ encouraged us to go there.

I think it's time to tell you a little bit about Russ.

Russ was a single-handed sailor on a very small boat, a twenty-seven foot Tartan named *Hygelig*. We had met him in New Zealand before setting off and marvelled at all that he had achieved in his small sloop. In a boat that was really designed to potter along the Great Lakes or day-hop the coast of the US, Russ had sailed the oceans of the world for twenty-one years. He was a professor of statistics before that, but, as he liked to say, had "seen the light" early and set off to cruise the world.

Along the way, his wife had been sated of the cruising life and so he continued on alone.

He jokes that she had said, "Russ, it's me or the boat!" and he had replied, "Good-bye honey!" True or not, it makes a good story and, the fact is, she returned to the US while he continued on alone. They are still great friends.

Russ was one of those sailors who wore his boat like a jacket. He was more a part of his boat than a master of it. He and his boat knew each other so well, were in such perfect harmony, that it was a joy to watch them sail together. I especially remember one time when we were approaching a very tricky passage through a shallow reef. The passage see-sawed through the coral with not much room to spare and no reliable navigation aids.

Chris and I were duly panicking . . . me up the ratlines shouting frantic instructions to Chris at the helm.

In front of us was Russ, calm as a cucumber. He made his way slowly and serenely through the coral, slowing down and leaving his helm on occasion to climb his mast and get a good look around, then descending and taking the helm again. Easy, peasy!

Russ had the cruising life sussed. He became our mentor and guide and our "training wheels" when we were first starting out.

Way back in New Zealand, when we first met him, Chris was asking him for any advice about cruising that he cared to share with us.

His reply was: "Well, first of all you have to know the rules of the cruising life, and one of the first of these rules is that cruising couples have a moral obligation to feed single-handed sailors."

He was, of course, joking. Nevertheless he spent many a dinner on *Skylark* in the next few months.

However, he also served us coffee most mornings. Out of practicality we were drinking instant coffee on board. Russ was horrified!

"Buying cheap sugar is frugal," he said. "Buying cheap coffee is just cheap."

Coffee was to be savoured as one of the pleasures in life. He ground his beans lovingly in a little brass Turkish coffee grinder and then used a plunger type coffee maker to brew the coffee. He then got in the dinghy with the freshly brewed hot coffee between his thighs and rowed over to *Skylark* to present us with the finished product.

Russ was also critical of our high energy levels. Chris and I, having spent years getting ready for this adventure, were still in high gear. We approached each new anchorage, each new destination with gusto and ran around immediately sussing out if there was a tourist office. We then proceeded to systematically see whatever there was to see as quickly and efficiently as possible.

Russ watched us in horror. "No . . . no . . . no . . . guys!" he said.

"The cruising life is all about taking it easy. You have left the rat race behind. You guys have to learn about sloth!"

His cruising life ran at a sedate pace. In the morning he would decide what he might want to do that day. Sometimes the day's activity might involve a swim. Just one swim . . . End of activities for that day.

We had much to learn. And we did listen and tried to slow down. After all, we were retired . . . What was the hurry? So . . . we sat in the cockpit and read our books.

Russ passed us in the dinghy and we proudly said, "Look, Russ...we are practicing sloth!"

"No . . . no . . . no," he replied, "If you have to practice it, you haven't got it right yet."

Anyway, here we were in Abemama, just the two boats, Russ and us.

He had been there three years before and was anxious to see if the local couple that he had befriended then was still around. As soon as we got ashore, they were there to greet us.

Rabina was a fisherman and spoke no English. His wife, Jean, however, had worked on another island for awhile and spoke some English. They invited us into their *bure,* a thatch-covered open raised platform that served as their living room. Close by were two other thatch- covered enclosures, these with walls of interwoven palm fronds. They served as kitchen/storage and sleeping quarters. All was beautifully situated on the pristine white sand that bordered the beach. Graceful, tall coconut palms provided shade. It was the kind of place that we had dreamed about in our wintry offices in New Zealand, in the years prior to departure.

Conversation in the *bure* was a little halting, due to the language barrier. Nevertheless, using a notebook to sketch out difficult concepts and a lot of hand movements, we made friends.

Somewhere in the conversation, Russ mentioned that it was my birthday that very day. Jean immediately left the *bure* to forage in the "bedroom hut" and came out with a beautiful hand-embroidered blouse and a colourful sarong as a present. I, of course, protested that gifts were not necessary. However, in the island culture, it would be an insult not to accept.

On top of that, Jean made it clear to us that we must show up on the island that evening for a *butaki* in my honour. She would organise it.

Suspicious foreigner that I am, I must admit that the thought crossed my mind that we would probably be charged for this party. Shame on me! I still had not understood the enormous generosity of these people. They have absolutely nothing except the coconuts, fish, breadfruit, and taro that God provides. But time and time again we were to see how generous they were with the little they had.

To please us, Jean used up her last bit of cooking oil to deep-fry thin slivers of breadfruit, because "foreigners like to eat it that way." The natives themselves eat it boiled.

Jean also spent three hours foraging on the reef at low tide to collect a bucketful of small cone-shells for us. She then boiled them and spent hours picking out the tasty morsels of meat from the shells. This was presented to me in a precious Tupperware container, which I did return filled with flour and sugar, items difficult to come by for islanders with little access to cash.

I tried to give gifts as well, but found that the more I gave the more she felt obliged to give. In their culture a gift warrants another gift, so I had to be careful to not let this get out of hand and deplete her of vital supplies.

So we spent a lovely morning relaxing in the *bure*. In the afternoon we returned to our boats to have a nap in preparation for the evening's party. Yes . . . we were starting to understand the concept of sloth!

We had asked Jean and Rabina what time to come for the party and they, looking a little perplexed, had nonetheless replied . . . about 7 p.m.

We also asked how long the party would go on, because we were a little worried about being able to return to our boats in the dinghy in the dark. The area was very tidal, and at low tide our boats and the shore were separated by several hundred metres of drying coral reef.

They indicated that we would probably be able to return to our boats by 10 p.m.

We did not know that time was a very fluid concept for them. There was at least one person on the island who had a watch or clock, because a sort of gong made of an old gas bottle and hung in a palm tree was banged with a hammer twice a day to alert the villagers that it was noon, and later 6 p.m. Other than that, time was estimated by the light of day.

We duly arrived at 7 p.m. and were escorted to an empty meeting house, which they were still decorating for the party.

They hurriedly went and fetched a mat woven from palm thatch and told us to be seated on it. It was a new mat, in our honour. And there we sat, for the next two hours, alone except for the occasional villager who was bringing flowers or leaves to provide decoration for the party.

The meeting house was a large open space under a thatch roof with low knee-high walls to allow the breeze through. The floor was covered in palm frond mats. However, in the corner, we saw a modern boom box connected to some kind of power source.

By about 9 p.m. the villagers started to arrive. The women each brought a large platter or container filled with all sorts of food. These were all placed in a line in front of us. Then each family took a seat at the edge of the hut opposite us. The proceedings started with a young girl bringing flower garlands and hanging them about our necks. She also placed a flower wreath on our heads.

Then there was a welcome from the chief of the village and then the police chief. They would stand up to address us at length and we nodded politely and smiled, though, of course, we had not understood a word.

Further speeches followed and each time they looked expectantly at us for an answer. In the end I stood up and thanked them for holding a party in my honour. This was translated by Jean, and for now, they seemed satisfied.

Following the speeches, I was given a plate and told to help myself from the long line of dishes provided by the women. The offerings were varied. There were all sorts of fish and shellfish, taro, breadfruit, even some rice. I was most intrigued by a very strange looking sea creature that kind of looked like a lobster-tail with a head attached. I thought I'd give it a go nonetheless, and it was very delicious. We later found out that it was a mantis shrimp. They live in the sand on the drying reef and are coaxed out of hiding by offering them a morsel of food on a stick.

Once I had helped myself, Chris and Russ were offered food.

Then the men helped themselves. The women and children sat quietly by while we ate. Once we were all finished, each woman retrieved what was left of her offering and shared it with her children.

After the meal, the entertainment started. Three beautiful little girls, about seven to nine years old, wearing flower wreaths on their heads, garlands around their necks, and a sort of skirt made from fresh leaves, danced for us. They smiled, swayed their hips, and made those incredibly graceful hand motions that the Pacific islands are famous for.

My heart almost ached with happiness. Here it was. Here we were. On a pristine Pacific island with these gorgeous children dancing their traditional dance, in the way their people had danced for centuries. Exactly this is what those seafarers of old also experienced. This is what inspired the romantic tales of the South Pacific that was to be the stuff of dreams for us northerners for centuries. I felt immeasurably privileged to experience this. What a birthday gift!

As the evening wore on, various groups danced or sang for us. Each time there seemed to be an expectation that we reciprocate with some kind of show, but of course, being ignorant foreigners and shy to boot, we had nothing to give. I again stood up and thanked them profusely for the great honour they had done me, but it felt inadequate. However, they are a generous people and seemed pleased with this small offering.

Then the dancing started.

Jean said, "Now we twist!"

The boom box started belting out dance music, both Western and Bollywood. People got up and started twirling around and bopping to their own version of modern dance.

We were not exempted, in fact being the guests of honour, we were asked to dance for every single dance to exhaustion. It was impossible to refuse. With sweat running down into every crevice, we did our best.

Soon, some of the women started to rush about among the dancers and spray us with what looked like deodorant. With great hilarity they aimed for armpits and crotches, giggling all the while. (We later found out that this was a tradition from the old days where the women would "freshen up" the sweaty dancers with perfumed oils.)

Next came the "powder game."

While, for instance, Chris was dancing with some old crone, one of the women would come up and put baby powder on his dance partner's cheek. She then had to try and catch Chris and put her cheek to his to transfer some of the powder to him. This was accompanied by shrieks of laughter as Chris, naturally, tried to avoid being powdered and ran around the dance floor with his partner in hot pursuit.

And so the evening went on.

There was no alcohol whatsoever involved. These people really knew how to enjoy themselves, and their stamina surprised us. Long after we were completely worn out, they were still going strong.

In the end, we excused ourselves and left them to it. It was by now 2 a.m. and our dinghy was stranded on the beach with what seemed like miles of dry coral reef between it and our boats. To boot, it was pitch black and we had only one tiny torch. We found small deeper channels in the reef here and there and dragged and sometimes carried the dinghy between them. I think it took us an hour to get back to the boats.

Still . . . what a night!

We remained in Abemama for about a week. During this time, I decided to reciprocate and invite Jean and Rabina for a meal on *Skylark*, to thank them for their incredible kindness and generosity to us.

I prepared all sorts of foods which I knew they would not have access to on their little island, and they seemed to enjoy it. They must have felt quite alien though. Our boats, our tiny little bits of Western culture, are a world apart from what they are used to. We often think of ourselves as rather poor, retired and living on a small pension. To them we must seem incredibly wealthy, with our boats full of modern gadgets, food, furniture, and entertainment.

After the meal, with the stilted conversation lagging a bit, Chris came upon the idea to show them a DVD on the laptop.

He chose David Attenborough's *Blue Planet*, and in particular the episode that deals with tropical oceans.

I will never forget their faces as they first looked on the images of this underwater world. I get goose pimples even thinking about it now. This was the very first time that they had a glimpse of what was under the water surrounding their island.

"Is it real?" asked Jean.

"It looks like a garden!"

Rabina, who had fished these waters all his life, kept pointing and exclaiming as he saw fish that he had pulled out of the ocean swimming about in their natural environment.

There was a sequence that showed a parrot fish eating off an underwater reef and then shitting out sand. The sand was shown to build up over time and create a beach. They both exclaimed loudly at this.

"Is this how our island was made?!" said Jean with astonishment.

Finally, it was time to think of departing from this island paradise.

But . . . not without another *butaki*. The villagers insisted on throwing us a good-bye party!

This time, however, we were prepared. We brought gifts,

deodorant, and baby powder, but more importantly, I cajoled the boys into preparing an entertainment. We decided to sing and dance along to Rod Stewart's "I Am Sailing." We stood in a row and sang along to the tune and invented hand movements to demonstrate the words. Kind of like one does in kindergarten, flapping our arms to the words "I am flying," etc. You get the picture. It was silly, and it was amateurish, but at least it was something. We practiced on the boat till we had it down pat. We also prepared song sheets with the words and recorded a copy of the song on a CD to leave with the villagers.

Our efforts were a great success. They loved it!

And they soon demonstrated their incredible ability to mimic by copying our actions almost immediately.

First the youngsters tried it. Then the police chief had a go, followed by the village chief and the pastor.

By the end of the evening the entire village stood in a circle with us and danced and sang to "I Am Sailing"!

I wondered about the next time a boat came to visit Abemama. Would they wonder how it was that Rod Stewart had come to this small dot in the Pacific? Would our little dance become one of their traditions? Who knows!

CHAPTER 10

The journey continued northwards through Kiribati and on to the Marshall Islands, another remote group of Pacific islands famous for the nuclear tests on Bikini Atoll.

We reached the Marshall Islands by Christmas, but did not stay long there. We had decided to carry on through Micronesia.

This is still a relatively unexplored part of the Pacific . . . You would say it is off the beaten track. Most yachts, when going westward toward Asia, will first head south and skirt Australia. They make their way through Torres Strait and on toward Bali and the Indonesian islands. This way you can almost day-hop your way north and west and eventually end up in the Malacca Straits, Singapore, Malaysia, and Thailand.

We chose a more direct and less travelled route, heading due west along the equator through Micronesia.

We left our "training wheels" in the Marshall Islands. Russ had made the grave error of looking at his bank statements, and decided he needed to top up the cruising kitty. He was able to get a job teaching English at the local college, so decided to remain there for a year or so.

It was painful to leave him. Not because we would miss his invaluable advice and sailing experience, which we would, but because he had become family. We had spent an intense year and a half together and his absence left a definite hole in our lives.

At the same time, I guess there was an excitement at being on our own. Especially as we were now heading into less travelled waters. We knew that we would rarely see another yacht in the next few months as we made our way through a group of islands called the Caroline Islands. We also knew that in the Caroline Islands we would find some of the most untouched island culture. Places where time had stood still, where people still lived very much like they had hundreds of years ago.

The Caroline Islands are a group of islands that used to be independent island kingdoms. After World War II, they were a US trust territory, but in 1986 four of these: Kosrae, Pohnpei, Truk, and Yap joined together and formed the Federated States of Micronesia. The most westerly island, Palau, became independent as late as 1994.

All of these island nations are remote, mysterious, and beautiful.

Kosrae is a single island covered in impossibly green, tropical, rainforest-clad hills.

Pohnpei is a cluster of low-lying palm-studded islets, one prettier than the next. We spent a week on one completely on our own, nothing but us, the beach, the palm trees, and the crystal clear water. Ant Atoll, it was called. A little piece of paradise, just for us. We did not produce much laundry that week!

Our next stop was the island nation of Yap. It consists of a myriad of picture-perfect coral islands. We chose to stop at one of them, called Lamotrek. It was to become another highlight of our cruising career. What a place!

As we negotiated our way through the outer reef and into the lagoon we noticed a small, graceful, local sailing canoe passing us, on its way out. It did not look like they were off for a day's fishing. It looked like they were headed off on a longer journey. We wondered at this, as the closest island, to our knowledge, was a very long way away, and especially a long way to go for a small canoe constructed of bamboo and coconut fibre with a woven palm-frond sail.

Later we asked about these sailors and were told that they were returning to their home island of Satawal forty miles away. They had run out of tobacco and had sailed to Lamotrek to see if they had any to spare. Alas, Lamotrek was tobacco-less as well, so they returned empty-handed. That is what I call a serious tobacco habit!

In the meantime, we found a spot to drop our anchor. As usual, we were the only yacht there.

It was another gorgeous island, with lush palm trees fringing the white sand beach. We could see a couple of canoes pulled up on the beach and some blue and red sarongs hung out to dry. Other than that, there was no indication that the island was even inhabited. There were no people in sight.

We prepared a gift pack. By now, we knew what would be appreciated by the natives. The islands and the ocean provide them with the basics, such as coconuts, taro, breadfruit, bananas, papaya, shellfish, and fish. They usually keep a few pigs and chickens for special occasions. However, they no longer live in complete isolation, so they have learned to covet outside things such as sugar, flour, rice, and tobacco. Any kind of canned goods are a real luxury, as are practical items such as fishing tackle, a diving mask, a pair of reading glasses. These they have to purchase . . . and therein lies the problem. How do you acquire cash on an island where there is no money to be earned?

On some of the larger islands there might be enough coconut

trees so that there is more than needed by the locals. These lucky islanders can sell a sack or two of copra and get money that way. But most of the islands are so small that they can only provide for the locals, and hardly even that. They have nothing to spare, nothing to sell. What cash there is comes from a relative who has gone to work on the main island or abroad, or from government hand-outs.

So . . . anything that we could contribute was greatly appreciated.

We launched the dinghy and headed ashore. As we were pulling the dinghy up out of the surf, we were approached by a sarong-clad, bare-chested middle-aged man. We asked if he spoke any English and he indicated that he understood some. We asked to be taken to the chief of his village. He nodded and asked us to wait.

Soon we were surrounded by men of all ages. They were all bare-chested and wearing sarongs. Some wore a solid blue sarong and others a solid red sarong. This seemed to be almost a uniform. Many had a wreath of flowers in their hair. I couldn't see any women at all, which I found curious. Usually, the women and children would be the first to approach us when we stepped foot on an island.

Anyway, soon the English-speaking man returned and asked us to follow him. He took us to a clearing where there were four palm trunks on the ground arranged in a square. A very old man sat on one of the palm trunks. He was obviously the chief. They indicated for Chris to sit near him, which he did, and handed our gift to the assistant. Chris did not try to shake his hand, as we did not know if this was customary here.

Chris was following a kind of protocol that we had been taught in Fiji some months earlier. We actually went on a course, arranged for yachties like us, to learn how to approach a native chief and ask for permission to stay.

There are ways to do this correctly and many, many no-nos. For instance, you never hand the gift directly to the chief. You do not speak to him unless spoken to first.

You speak through the assistant and ask for permission to anchor in his waters, to step on his shore, and to visit his village. You always sit in a position below or in front of the chief. You must not show him the soles of your feet, so you must sit cross-legged. In Fiji you have to bring a bundle of kava (a root which is a mild drug) with you, which is given to the chief. He twirls it in his hands and considers whether he will grant you the request.

Eventually he claps his hands and says "You may anchor in my water. You may step on my beach. You may visit my village. You may drink our water. You are now a member of my family, and we will protect you and care for you."

They mean it too! Once you have been accepted, they feel responsible for you. If an accident should befall you while you are with them, they will do everything in their power to get help.

Of course, we were now in Lamotrek, in Micronesia, and many, many miles from Fiji. We had no idea what the proper protocol was on this island, but it seemed prudent to use more or less the same approach.

I guess we got it somewhat right, because fairly soon there was a welcome forthcoming and everyone relaxed.

In our gift pack was one packet of cigarettes. Chris and I are not smokers and we debated whether we should even be encouraging smoking by bringing cigarettes as a gift. However, we had heard from other cruisers that tobacco of any kind was very precious to the islanders in Micronesia, so we relented and brought some along.

As it turns out, they don't smoke the tobacco. They are all very fond of chewing betel nut, and although you can prepare a packet of betel nut without tobacco, apparently it enhances the "chew" if you sprinkle some tobacco on the leaf.

The chief duly opened the packet of cigarettes and handed a single cigarette to each of the men present. They, in turn, would take the cigarette apart and distribute the precious strands of tobacco to their entire family.

Once we were accepted as "honoured guests" by the chief, everyone crowded around us and our interpreter did his best to introduce us to the men.

There were still no women in the area and I asked about this. He explained that we were at the moment in the "men's area" and women were not permitted there. The square formed by the palm logs was, in fact, a kind of meeting/drinking area for the men. They spent most of their days there drinking and chatting.

As we were soon to learn, drinking was about all the men did on Lamotrek. The only interruption to their drinking was to climb a palm tree in the morning to collect the "palm wine" for the afternoon's drinking session and to climb a palm tree in the afternoon to collect the "palm wine" for the next morning's drinking session.

On occasion they also went fishing . . . a task assigned to men which was taboo for women. It was considered bad luck to even look at a woman before going off fishing and woe betide any woman who handled fishing equipment or even wished a man good luck for the day's fishing.

Of course, I realized that I had already put my proverbial foot in it, as I had cheerfully wished some fishermen good luck that same morning.

They must have cringed! I apologised as the ignorant boor that I was, but our host assured us that these rules did not apply to foreign women.

We were somehow considered a breed apart. For this reason I was also allowed into the men's area.

I soon removed myself from there though and went in search of the women. Chris, in the meantime, spent most of the next week in a faintly befuddled drunken haze. No sooner had he been offered a drink in one palm trunk square (their idea of the local pub) when he was called over to the next palm trunk square two hundred metres further down the beach. His memories of Lamotrek consist mainly of the Lamotrek version of the "pub crawl."

I, however, did find the women. They had been there all along, skirting an invisible line which marked the edge of the men's area.

The women also wore a kind of uniform, or at least, the lower part of a uniform. They were as bare-chested as the men, but instead of a blue or red sarong they wore a kind of knee-high kilt of multicoloured stripes. Fat babies with flower wreaths in their hair dangled from their hips or cowered behind their legs.

Again I was struck by that "Wow!" feeling. Here were the brown-skinned bare-breasted beauties from the sea shanties of old. They were beautiful . . . until they opened their mouths in smiled greeting. Almost all of them had red or blackened teeth, a result of their betel nut chewing habit.

Among the women I also found a friend who spoke a little English. Her name was Esther and she was as bare-chested as the rest of them, but she had been off their little island and spent time on the capital island of Yap, learning some English and some medical skills.

She was the island medic and proudly showed me her "dispensary," a hut containing a cupboard marked with a red cross. Inside were a few bandages, Band-Aids, Dettol, and aspirin.

She took me to her hut and offered me a young coconut to drink. Soon I was surrounded by "the girls" and we swapped stories as best we could.

Turns out that a woman's lot on Lamotrek is a fairly tough one. While the men . . . well . . . drink all day, the women do pretty much all the rest. They look after the home and kids, they tend the taro plantation and the pigs, they weave their sarongs and kilts on bamboo looms, they cook, bake, clean, wash clothes . . . Sound familiar? Still, they seemed quite content, all the same.

At one point Esther took Chris and me on a tour of the island. There was a path made of crushed coral that ran through the middle and around the edges of the island. The whole island was perhaps a couple of miles long and a mile wide, so it did not take long to see it all.

Whenever our tour took us close to a native dwelling, Esther did a curious thing. She would call out when we were still a bit of a distance from the dwelling. Depending on the reply, she would either proceed past the house walking as normal, or she would adopt a crouching position with her head well down, almost as though she were cowering, anticipating a blow.

When asked about this, she explained that she was calling to see if there were any male members of the family at home. If there were, she had to show respect of the males, by adopting the crouching stance while walking past.

Wow! I guess women's lib has yet to make inroads on Lamotrek!

Despite these cultural differences, or perhaps because of them, we found the stay on Lamotrek to be an incredible experience.

Again we were struck by the enormous generosity of the locals. They were almost competing with each other to provide us with gifts of bananas, coconuts, and flower wreaths. I was told that it took a woman about three weeks to weave one of their beautiful kilts. By the time we left, I had received three of these as gifts. All payment for them was adamantly refused. They represented nine weeks of work!

We were able to reciprocate in small ways though.

The men asked Chris to look at a broken stud on an outboard motor block. Could he fix it?

He tried his best to find a replacement on board, unsuccessfully, but he was able to drill it out for them.

Yes, they did have outboard motors, or at least a couple of people did. However, the supply ship that usually visited every three months or so had broken down. They had not had a supply ship for over six months and were short of everything. For instance, they had long since run out of fuel for the outboards. This was serious, as there were not that many sailing canoes left and they could not fish without them. They were in the process of building a new one, and we observed the men at the drinking sessions hand-sewing a sail.

In the end someone shyly asked whether we might have a sewing machine on board.

We did . . . so . . . a delegation of six very serious-looking men came out to the boat and I sat and sewed the seams for them where they indicated. A job that would have taken them weeks was completed in about an hour.

We also noticed that, except for a few cooking fires, the island was completely dark after nightfall. The women explained that they had run out of lamp-oil and although coconut oil could be used, they did not as yet have a large enough supply in place to replace the lamp-oil that they were used to. They asked if we had any spare diesel as this could be used in the lamps.

Even though diesel was a commodity that was precious to us as well, there being no possibility to refuel for several thousand miles, we did leave them with a twenty litre container to share among all the villagers.

I also invited Esther out to the boat.

In our conversations about what women do, I had mentioned that I had a machine that baked bread. She was very curious about this, so I decided to have her out to *Skylark* for a girl's bread-baking session.

She was dressed in her usual bare-breasted outfit, and as bread-baking is a hot activity, I soon felt overdressed in my   T-shirt and shorts.

When in Rome . . . and all that, I thought as I took my top off. Chris took a lot of photographs that day!

Alas, soon it was time to move on. We would have loved to stay longer than a week, but we were in a bit of a race against weather.

This part of Micronesia and the Philippines is famous for tropical cyclones. We were on a mission to reach Borneo before the cyclone season got going in earnest in late March. And we still had several thousand miles to go.

For our farewell, we were bedecked with several wreaths around our heads and necks, each family wanting to contribute to the good-bye. Esther painted our cheeks with coconut oil, coloured yellow with turmeric, for good luck. Our dinghy was filled with coconuts and two whole bunches of bananas.

As we weighed anchor, we felt privileged to have experienced this island where the local culture and traditions were still so intact.

As cruisers we constantly feel that it is a race against time. Western influences have made themselves felt in so many places already. So far, DVDs were a mystery to Lamotrek, but no doubt they would soon make their appearance. Instead of weaving flower wreaths, the youngsters would dream of fast cars and shiny PlayStations. And with that would come the dissatisfaction of not having what others have. What a shame!

However, on this day, they were happy, excited by the small change to their lives that our visit had provided, and yet, still content in their way of life.

CHAPTER 11

The last stop in Micronesia was Palau. Here the pace of life was very different. The island had only gained independence in 1994, having been a US trust territory since the war. The American influence was easy to see. There were hotels, restaurants, lots of cars, supermarkets, an airport, etc. It reminded me of some of the islands in the Caribbean that I had lived on in my twenties.

Having said that, it was a very lovely place. Nature wise, it was stunning. The larger islands were surrounded by a myriad of small coral islets set in crystal clear warm tropical water. These provided unending private anchoring possibilities. There were also reefs everywhere, the mainstay of the island economy. Palau is a diver's paradise. Fortunately, it is too remote to attract all but the most persistent tourists. Getting there is expensive, so you really have to want to. We needed to pay a visit to the UK in the very near future, and we seriously thought about leaving the boat in Palau. However, the airfares put us off. Horrendous! Instead, we spent a couple of weeks enjoying some of the best diving of our lives, and then set off on our last Pacific leg, heading toward the Philippines.

From now on, our cruising experience would always have a small, though very small, background aura of possible danger, not from reefs or winds, but from pirates, thieves, or terrorists.

One of us said, "We are heading into civilisation!" As soon as we said it, we both looked at each other and shook our heads.

"No." "Civilisation" is what we were leaving behind.

The simple, honest, generous people of the Pacific Islands were to our minds far more "civilised" than the more "sophisticated" nations we were about to encounter. Modern life and all its trappings seem to breed greed, stress, political and religious conflicts, and, most of all, dissatisfaction. And yet we are all drawn to it somehow, for the conveniences it provides us with.

We were as guilty as the next person. After months in paradise, we were looking forward to a hot shower, a marina, a proper chandlery, and a steak meal. From now on though, we would start to worry about things, like whether it was safe to leave our dinghy unattended, whether we might be boarded by thieves in the night, or simply whether we should keep our cash hidden and keep it in a bum bag (attached to our waist under our clothes) when going ashore. Sad, really sad, and such a contrast to the Pacific.

In the countries we were about to visit, there were a lot of very poor people. But, throughout the Pacific, to our standards, they were also very poor. There was a difference, however. The islanders had few possessions, but there was an equality in their poverty. Everyone on the island was in the same position. Sure, perhaps the chief might have a bigger hut and more power. But, ultimately they all shared the same coconuts, breadfruit, and fish. If you did not have food, it was their culture to share what they had. If your house fell down, the whole village got together and built you a new one. And I don't think they saw themselves as poor. They would marvel at our boat and all the cool stuff we had, and be extremely grateful to receive a present. But I think it was more a delight at something unusual, a novelty. It wasn't anything that they coveted or felt the need to have. I may be naïve and what I say may not be universally true for the entire Pacific, but that is how I perceived the island culture.

In Asia, it is different. Here there is a poverty that is more desperate. There are so many people; you cannot easily live off the land. And there is an inequality to their poverty. There are the many poor but also the few very rich. The poor see how the rich live and they want that life. They covet the things the rich have. Owning a dinghy or an outboard can make the difference between your family starving, or fish on the table. Desperate times require desperate measures. Unfortunately for us, this meant being more careful to protect ourselves and our things.

But first we had to get into the Philippines safely. This meant passing very close to a known bastion of piracy, Mindanao Island.

The Philippines is an island nation. It consists of an archipelago of some large, but hundreds of small, islands. These are surrounded by channels or straits of varying size where the tide is concentrated into amazingly strong tidal flows. There are also plenty of reefs and overfalls. All in all a challenging area.

Approaching from the southeast, the logical entrance into this maze of islands was via Surigao Strait. Unfortunately the Strait veers south and narrows into a gap just ten miles across. On one side you have the reputedly safe island of Leyte. On the other side, however, you have the reputedly unsafe pirate stronghold of Mindanao. How unsafe it was, we did not know. Apparently the island had a history of piracy. Added to that, there was talk of religious and political strife between predominantly Muslim Mindanao and the rest of the Philippines which is mainly Catholic. In any case, we had been told that it was a place to avoid at all cost.

Getting within ten miles of a pirate stronghold is no laughing matter. Ten miles is nothing. In a skiff with a fast outboard, it would take less than half an hour to reach us from shore. So we were worried. Some said to plan your arrival so that you would pass this bottleneck at night. However, we did not relish the thought of travelling through reef-infested waters with a strong current in the middle of the night. We had also heard that there were literally hundreds of small unlit fishing craft at night. So we decided to approach in daylight and go as close to the safe shore as possible. In the end we saw neither hide nor hair of anything resembling a pirate. Phew!

The next adventure was trying to clear into the country. Because of the strong currents, which can flow up to ten knots against you, navigating in the Philippines is a matter of choosing your moment to hop from place to place. As you really want to do your sailing during daylight hours, this can mean having to wait in an anchorage for a day or two until the timing of the tides is right. For these reasons, and because there are very few places which are a Port of Entry, we had been told not to worry too much if we needed to spend a week or two in Philippine waters before checking in.

This however, went against our grain. Chris and I are really a pair of "goody two shoes," the one worse than the other. We were both model students at school, nerds really, and we still hate to bend the rules. So we poured over our *Cruising Guide*, to see where the first available Port of Entry might be. The book said we could check in at a place called Maasin.

It still took us a couple of days to get there, but we duly arrived at Maasin and put up our yellow quarantine flag, to signify that we were a foreign yacht just arriving in the country. It wasn't much of a bay, in the sense that it was hardly an indentation in the coast, but there was a reef providing some shelter, and there was another yacht anchored there. There was also no beach, only a rubbish-strewn shoreline with ramshackle houses which seemed to overhang the water in most places. The predominant feature of the place was a huge statue of the Virgin Mary looking down at you from her perch atop the hill.

We launched the dinghy and made our way over to the other yacht, to see if we could get a little local knowhow. The yacht looked rather the worse for wear, but we did not hold that against her. After the many miles in the Pacific without a marina, *Skylark* did not look that shipshape either.

Our calls of "Ahoy there!" resulted in the appearance of a tousled, long-haired grey head with a huge welcoming smile.

The ageing skipper, a Welshman, Ivor, who we would have

judged to be in his seventies, was joined in the cockpit by his Filipino "lady love" of a decidedly later vintage, perhaps twenty at most.

Now, now . . . don't be quick to judge, I told myself. Live and let live. To each his own . . . etc., etc.

Anyway, after welcoming us to the Philippines, Ivor told us, in his delightful sing-song Welsh accent, that our book must be wrong. He did not think we could check in at Maasin.

"Wait till Cebu City! No one will mind!"

He, himself, apparently, did not bother too much about that sort of thing. "I tell the local Coast Guard I'm here, and leave it at that!"

Still, he told us where to park our dinghy safely.

"See the local lads that are drinking under that blue tarpaulin? Pull your dinghy up there and they'll keep an eye on it. Just tell them you know me and buy them a beer."

The "tavern" of the blue tarpaulin (which it turns out that Ivor had donated to the guys so they would not have to drink in the sun) led down a filthy narrow alley, past deteriorating wooden shacks and outdoor hearths and into the busy main street of Maasin. Our senses were assaulted by the noise, the hustle and bustle of cycle rickshaws, cars, trucks, and people, people, people. It was very different from where we had come from, and this was just a small town!

We wandered around, trying to find an official-looking building, because despite Ivor's advice to the contrary, we still hoped to check in.

Finally we saw a building, much in need of a new paint job, with "Immigration" painted in black letters above the door.

We went in and announced to the couple of ladies sat at a desk, "We are from a yacht and have just arrived in the Philippines!"

Blank stares. We tried again.

"Here are our passports. You are Immigration? We need a stamp."

Blank stares. Finally one of the ladies indicated that we should wait and got on the phone. She was obviously speaking to a superior about these strange people that had just walked in her door, and the upshot of the conversation was that

"You must go Tacloban!"

"Okay," we said. "No problem." "Where is Tacloban?"

We gestured out the door, thinking it might be some other part of the town.

"No, no, not here, other place."

"Okay," we said. "Can we go there by boat?"

They nodded.

"How far?" They conferred for a while among themselves and came up with that it would take an hour or so by boat, but it would be better to take the bus in the morning. They showed us where the bus station was and told us the bus left at 8 a.m.

Foolishly, based on their estimate of time it would take to get there by boat, we assumed the place to be a few miles distant, an easy bus ride.

We showed up at 8 a.m. the next morning, passports and boat papers in hand, and caught the bus marked Tacloban. It was a slow ride, the bus stopping in every village and hamlet. After about an hour, we decided to ask the driver how much further it would be to Tacloban. To our dismay, we were told that we would get to Tacloban by 1 p.m.! It was a five hour bus ride away!

As it turned out, we would have only two hours to spare in Tacloban, because the return bus left at 3 p.m. and if we missed it, we would not only have to spend the night, but leave our boat unattended.

To top things off, it started to rain torrentially when we got there. It was also a very large place, and we had no clue where the Immigration office might be. We resorted to a tuk-tuk, a motorised rickshaw, and after a few false leads the driver did find the correct place.

So far, so good. However, the officials wanted copies of everything and in triplicate, and no . . . they did not have a photocopier . . . Why should they? They also wanted a quite considerable "service fee" (in essence a bribe) to check us in, and for this we needed an ATM.

Small problem, the ATMs in Tacloban would not accept our cards, although they had worked just fine in an ATM in much smaller Maasin.

We scraped together our last pennies to have the required photocopies made and returned to the Immigration office. By this time we were absolutely soaked to the skin and stood there in the Immigration office making large wet puddles on the floor. They took pity on us in the end, and decided to give us the stamps in our passport, as long as we promised to go to the Immigration office in Maasin and pay the "service fee" the next day.

We made it to the bus just in time, and had a miserable long journey back in our wet clothes.

And we had not even cleared Customs yet. But by this stage, we could see the wisdom in not being too fussy about sticking to the rules.

"Sod that! We'll do the rest of the clearance in Cebu City, whenever we get there!"

We did not linger for very long in the Philippines. They say that there are some wonderful spots there and I'm sure that is correct. However, it is also the country with the highest incidence of hurricanes in the world, and we found that a bit off-putting. We were there in early March, which is quiet in terms of hurricanes, but the season would start in earnest in a few weeks. There are people who spend years cruising the Philippines, and they say it is not a problem, as there are very many very safe anchorages there, so called "hurricane holes."

But, as our friend Fatty Goodlander says, "The problem with hurricane holes is that when there is a hurricane it is still in there with you."

Speaking of Fatty, it turned out that he and Carolyn were in the Philippines at the same time as us. We were in touch by email and Fatty told us that he was anchored in a bay called Port Bonbonon, an extraordinary place, full of scruffy yachts belonging to "Eurotrash and Americans-under-indictment."

It sounded intriguing, so we headed to meet up with them. We found Fatty on his own on *Wild Card*, with Carolyn away in Hong Kong on a purchasing trip. Poor Fatty was ill with a tropical fever, so I provided "meals on keels" for the next week, to help nurse him back to health.

Fatty was right, it was an interesting place. I guess the most striking feature was that it was populated by scruffy sailors, mostly single-handers and mostly getting on in years. The bay was almost a retirement home for ageing male cruisers.

The attraction? You guessed it . . . Almost every yacht had one or more young attractive Filipino ladies working above (and below) decks. I remember thinking, while walking down the marine promenade of the nearby town of Dumaguete, passing bar after bar filled with older men and their beautiful young partners, that they must pity poor Chris, stuck as he was with a woman on his arm only seven years his junior.

We soon weighed anchor and headed for the relatively hurricane-free waters of Borneo.

CHAPTER 12

Leaving the Philippines we again had to be careful not to stray into pirate waters. This time, the place to avoid was the Sulu Archipelago. We were crossing the Sulu Sea, but we kept the dicey area well to our south and headed for the northernmost tip of Borneo.

However, I remember feeling a bit wary during this trip. I kept looking to port, hoping not to see any kind of vessel coming from that direction. At the time, I still did not distinguish between "good" pirates and "bad" pirates, the way I do now. After our experience in the Indian Ocean, which was still a couple of years in our future, these guys in the Sulu Archipelago would have been categorised as "good" pirates. Meaning . . . they would probably rob you if they got the chance, but they were not that likely to take you hostage or kill you, like the Somali pirates do.

But I am getting ahead of myself. First let me tell you a little about Borneo.

We arrived in Kudat, a small fishing town in Malaysian Borneo.

I was so excited about Borneo! I had watched plenty of National Geographic specials about this place and imagined it as a wild place of virgin jungle and orang-utans. I guess I was a little disappointed.

Kudat looked pretty much like any small Asian fishing town. Not a jungle in sight! Our *Cruising Guide* urged caution in this area, I suppose because it was still a bit close to the Sulu Archipelago and those pirates. This was also our first stop in a Muslim country. So we did not know quite what to expect.

What we got was pure and simple, genuine hospitality.

When we first stepped ashore to look for the Immigration and Customs office, an older woman in a long flowing gown and headscarf, lower face covered, made a beeline for us, crossing the road, and appearing to shout at us.

We wondered what was going to happen, but she gave us a huge smile, held out her hand and said, in English, "Welcome to Kudat!"

This pretty much summed up the place. Everyone treated us with the utmost courtesy and friendliness. We had also never before had a clearing-in procedure where the Immigration Officer drove us to the Customs office in his own car and waited for us, later to drive us back to the boat. They were just so nice, that I forgot all about the lack of jungle.

In fact, there is plenty of jungle in Borneo, just not all over. Sadly, commercial interests rule, and a lot of the beautiful virgin forest has been chopped down to make way for palm oil plantations. Still, you can find the jungle when you want to, and we would later spend three very exciting nights in a primitive jungle camp right in the middle of the virgin forest with orang-utans, proboscis monkeys, tarantulas . . . the lot.

But first we wanted a bit of rest. We had sailed a lot of miles from the Marshall Islands to Borneo, constantly egging ourselves on and not daring to stop anywhere too long. We just did not want anything to do with a hurricane, and we had made it! Time for a little R&R.

We thought we would go check out a place we had heard about, Sutera Harbour Marina, a bit further down the coast in Kota Kinabalu. This is the capital of Malaysian Borneo, and was reputed to be a terrific place to spend a little time.

Now, Chris and I are definitely not marina people, I think more by necessity than choice. We simply cannot afford to stay in marinas and prefer to swing on our own anchor and spend our funds on other things. Not that there had been much choice in the Pacific. There just weren't any marinas around.

However, we had heard that Sutera Harbour was not an experience to be missed, so we said "Okay, we'll make an exception, and stay for a week." Three months later, we were still there!

It was just too good to be true! At the risk of sounding like a travel brochure . . . the place was amazing. On either side of the central luxurious Sutera Harbour Yacht Club, there were two seven star hotels. You had a choice of three swimming pools, one Olympic size; there was a gym, tennis courts, squash courts, golf course, numerous restaurants and bars, air-conditioned changing rooms, a movie theatre showing free movies on weekends, etc., etc. On top of that, there was a free air-conditioned, hourly shuttle bus taking you into downtown Kota Kinabalu, just minutes away. All this for less than the price of our marina berth in New Zealand.

So . . . we splurged, and relaxed and had a marvellous time! And ate, and ate and ate.

We had hardly been to a restaurant in over a year. Now we had a whole charming town full of them.

Kota Kinabalu is predominantly Chinese Malaysian, and this is reflected in the food offerings. Pretty much every corner of every street had a *kedai kopi,* a coffee shop. These not only served coffee, tea, and sometimes beer, they usually rented out space to specialty food booths. For a tiny bit of money, you could eat the most gorgeous meals such as laksa, stir-fries, stews, dim sum, chicken and rice, etc., etc.

We were lucky in another way too. My brother is married to Rema, his Indian Malaysian wife, and they live in Kuala Lumpur. When she heard that we would be in Kota Kinabalu, she immediately contacted a childhood family friend, a Malaysian Chinese, Mr. Murphy Wong, who lived there. He was given the assignment to look after us, and did so most excellently. In fact, the Wongs pretty much adopted us while we were there.

Murphy would call us daily and say, "Where are you chaps?"

Then he would tell us to come to this *kedai kopi* or the other because, "They make the best buns in town and you must be there at 3 p.m. to get them fresh!"

In fact, while we were there, my brother Ole, his wife, and her brother all came to visit us on the boat. It was crowded, but fun, especially as Rema and her brother Ravi, who looks a bit like Gandhi, were very unlikely live-aboards. I think they were sort of expecting the *Queen Mary* and a bit shocked at the confined spaces of life aboard. But they took it all in good spirit, especially Ravi, who delighted us by his keen interest in everything nautical.

Rema, too, came up trumps when she talked some local fishermen into trading a six-pack of beer for over three kilos of prawns. There is nothing like having a local around when bartering for stuff! At the market Rema would ask us what we wanted to purchase and then tell us to "Go hide your white faces . . . and leave this to me!"

Eventually, we had to start getting serious again. The boat needed fresh bottom paint and a few repairs. We headed back to Kudat and the scruffy commercial boat yard there. It was rough, but it would do. They had a travel-lift.

They also had a lot of dogs, puppy dogs. Malaysian Muslims don't like dogs; they are regarded as unclean. Chinese Malaysians, perhaps as a protest, love dogs. This boatyard was owned by a Chinese, so he had a lot of dogs . . . for security. Two of the bitches had just given birth, so there were puppies absolutely everywhere.

Next door to the boatyard was a mosque. So, there we were, spending our first night "on the hard," sleeping on the boat while she was out of the water. Dawn broke and the muezzin started his call, loudly from a loudspeaker.

"Allahu Akbar!"

Immediately his call was answered by a very loud chorus of howling dogs. It was impossible to sleep through. We looked at the clock . . . 5 am . . . and just giggled. This was to be our wake-up call for the next couple of months.

We ended up leaving the boat in Kudat while we took a trip back to the UK for a short visit.

When we left New Zealand, I had dreamed about just sailing off into the sunset, not a care in the world. But . . . there is that "but" again. None of us are immune to the cares of the world. Most of us have family and, if we are lucky, they want us and need us on occasion.

Chris' Dad was in his nineties and living on his own on the Isle of Wight. His mother has been in a home for a long time. His sister and brother cared for Dad, but they needed a break once in a while. Chris also has two grown sons, who want him in their lives. In short, we had family obligations. So, once in a while we had to put our cruise on hold for a couple of months, and head back to the UK to do our bit.

In the end, I think this actually enhanced our cruising experience. Even living your dream can become par for the course after a while, and the breaks on land made it all the sweeter when we got back.

In this case, going back meant going back to life in a dusty boatyard.

Again, if you want to follow your dreams, there is always a cost. For me one of the worst parts of the cruising life was the times when we had to take the boat out of the water to paint the bottom. This would usually be a bit of a hardship as we would live on the boat while working on it. "Living on the hard," we call it in cruising circles.

It's not terribly romantic. You find yourself three meters off the ground in a dusty, dirty, industrial environment, usually with very basic facilities. If you are lucky there is a loo close by. If you are very lucky there is also a shared shower.

In one place where we spent four months on the hard, on the island of Langkawi, Malaysia, the shower consisted of a hose hung on a chain link fence . . . and this in a Muslim country. For a woman, that meant trying to wash under your clothes in full view of spectators. The loo was an Asian squat toilet and that was located about five hundred meters away. I used to take the hired motorbike to go to the loo. I was certainly not game to cross five hundred meters of boatyard in my jammies at night . . . so . . . yep . . . at night there was the bucket. In the mornings, Chris, my knight in shining armour, added waste disposal to all his other jobs.

But . . . as a cruiser . . . you take all of that with as much humour as you can muster. It is the price we pay for the good times.

However, even here in the boatyard in Kudat, there was the joy of meeting new people. Alongside our boat there was a charming Australian couple, also living on their boat, and we became firm friends. There was also a young Englishman, building the boat of his dreams. He worked in the merchant navy as a navigation officer on a cable-laying boat.

He told us horrendous stories of near collisions with small sailing boats. If we did not know it before, he instilled in us the absolute need to watch out for and get out of the way of big ships. He said that these days there was so much paperwork for the officer on watch to complete that they rarely looked out the window when on passage. Instead the big ships relied on radar to advise them of anyone else out there.

As a sailboat is very small, we are often not a good radar target and can easily be missed. Might is right and if we wanted to avoid a collision, we needed to be constantly alert.

CHAPTER 13

One of the things that I really love about the cruising life is the contrasts. Cruising one area of the world is like chalk and cheese to cruising another. Cruising the South Pacific is a totally different experience from cruising in South East Asia. Each area has a different beauty, a different experience, and a different set of challenges.

The South Pacific was all about remoteness, white sandy beaches, crystal clear water and primitive island culture. It was also about doing without: doing without marinas, chandleries, good supermarkets. It was about making do, on your small island of sophistication; it was about managing without. The prize was huge. Because you had your own boat, you got to see places most tourists can never see.

Cruising South East Asia, on the other hand, was more about using your boat as a relatively inexpensive transport vehicle and mobile hotel room to explore places other tourists could only reach by land or air transport, while staying in expensive hotels. Pretty much everywhere you go with a sailboat in South East Asia, the tourists can go too. They just have to pay more to get there. For us cruisers, it was now more about seeing things on land. Our cruising revolved around finding a safe place to park the boat while we hit the tourist spots. Land based guide books like *The Lonely Planet* took precedence in our lives over *Cruising Guides*.

We were also more dependent on marinas. There is always the threat of theft in the back of your mind, so you are reluctant to anchor just anywhere. By necessity exploring on land meant leaving our boat, or dinghy, on its own for extended periods of time. This could only really be done safely by parking in a marina. In terms of the local population, we were now regarded as the super-rich. And the super-rich in South East Asia are surrounded by security, to keep out the riff-raff. Whatever your opinion about this, this is just how it is. If you own an expensive toy like a yacht, you need to keep it safe in a marina with security guards on the perimeter.

This new lifestyle also had other repercussions. For the first time, we really felt the heat. Sure, it had been hot in the Pacific, but there had always been a cooling breeze. We were also always anchored, presenting the bow of the boat to the breeze. With a few hatches open, this funnelled air through the boat. And if you really got hot, there was beautiful clean water all around for a cooling swim.

Things were different in Southeast Asia. First of all, the breeze was often nonexistent. However, even when there was a breeze, we were now mostly berthed in marinas, thus not presenting the bow to the wind. The natural air-conditioning provided by our hatches was out of play. Jump over the side to cool off? Well . . . not really. Most of the harbours and marinas were pretty polluted. Fortunately a lot of marinas had swimming pools, providing some relief.

For all these reasons, we started to see the phenomenon of the cruising "cave-dweller." These were cruisers who had obviously been in this area for awhile. They had succumbed to purchasing an air-conditioner. Not a yacht-specific one. They are enormously expensive and you only really see them on the very flash yachts. No . . . they had purchased an air-conditioning unit meant for housing. Typically they had mounted it over one of their hatches. In this way, they could close down their hatches and enjoy air-conditioned comfort on their boat. The only problem was that this pretty much forces you to stay only in marinas, because of the huge power draw. You also tend to stay below in your boat, eliminating life in the cockpit, and all the easy socializing with other cruisers. We hardly ever saw the people who lived like this . . . They were "cave-dwellers."

Nonetheless, despite these drawbacks, cruising South East Asia is still a fantastic experience. We thoroughly enjoyed the Asian culture and exploring the sights. There were temples, museums, wildlife sanctuaries, a trip into the jungle, bustling markets, incredible and inexpensive food, and lots of weird and wonderful things that you could not find anywhere else in the world.

There was also the odd, off-lying island, where there was a sandy beach and a relaxed anchorage. However, you had to pick your time. Almost always there would be a tourist boat arriving with swarms of tourists at some point in the day. Some of the islands had also been turned into hideously expensive resorts and to them, we cruisers were the riff-raff, the poor cousins of their wealthy clients, and we were unceremoniously told to move on, no anchoring in their pristine bay.

So we made our way down the coast of Borneo and arrived in Brunei, home to the Sultan of Brunei, one of the richest men in the world. Brunei had a lot to offer in the way of lovely mosques and chrome and glass architecture, but my memories of our stay there will always centre on Ben the rat.

We had been told to be careful of rats. They would climb aboard a boat in a marina, but apparently even at anchor, you weren't safe, as they could swim out to the boat and climb your anchor-chain.

This last bit, I had always put down to hysteria. I quite frankly did not believe it.

I was wrong. Because . . . Ben swam to the boat . . . We know he did!!!

It is not hard to know when you have a rat on board a small boat. It's pretty obvious: chew marks on your veggies, rustling at night. He can't hide for long. So we knew exactly when he had come aboard, and it was while we were at anchor, at least a hundred meters from shore. In addition to this, we knew he had not snuck into the dinghy and got aboard that way, because we had not used the dinghy in this particular harbour. There were water taxis, and these would pick us up from our stern platform, with their bows hardly touching our boat, so he could not have come that way either. He definitely swam out to the boat and climbed the anchor chain! I stand corrected!

In any case, he soon made his presence known, and it was shortly after arrival in the anchorage outside the Brunei Yacht Club.

I was horrified! I just could not bear the thought that I was sharing a thirty-nine foot boat with a rat! We had not seen him, but the big bites taken out of the potatoes and tomatoes told a very clear story.

We had no means on board to trap him or kill him, so we went ashore to find someone who might be able to advise us what to do. One of the other cruisers there had experience of this, and told us to go into the little town and buy a trap, a wire cage with a tripping device on the door. He also told us to eliminate all other food sources, so the rat would be forced to go for the bait in the trap.

So, this is what we did. While Chris set up the trap in the area where we had found the nibbled veggies, I went around the boat and collected all our food and put it in a large plastic storage bag, which I hung in the cockpit.

We were really worried. It was not just a matter of finding it distasteful to share our space with a rat. It could be a potential disaster. Rats have been known to chew their way through electric cables, disabling a yacht's electronics and navigation gear. We had to get rid of the problem, and quickly!

Once the trap was set, we went ashore for a drink. A few hours later, we got back to the boat and checked the trap. The rat had been in there and taken the bait! But . . . we had not set the trap correctly. The door had got hung up and the rat had escaped, probably frightened silly, and now disinclined to go anywhere near that trap again. Bugger!

Off to town again, to buy trap number two. We left the first one where it was and put the new one close by.

I had now also been given a lesson in rat psychology, by our rat-experienced cruising friends. Apparently it was important to make the rat feel comfortable about the cage.

"Put something soft in there, so its little feet have something soft to walk on."

"Rats don't like open spaces. They don't like feeling that they can be observed while eating. Cover the roof of the cage, so he feels safe."

They reckoned that our rat would now be spooked, so we needed to give it confidence.

"Put a slice of bread about half a meter from the cage. Let it take this safely the first night. The next night move it closer to the cage, and so on. You must train the rat to get into the cage!"

Bloody hell! Was there no end to the skills we had to acquire to be successful cruisers? Now we had to be rat trainers too!

But we did as they suggested.

On the first night, I found that he ignored the bread, because he had found the bag with our food that I had suspended in the cockpit. He must have leapt a couple of feet to get there, but sure enough, there was a hole in the side of the bag and nibbles taken out of the biscuits!

Ok, *now it was war!* I took the bag to the bow of the boat and attached it to one of the halyards. I hoisted the whole thing up so that the bag was dangling some three metres above the deck and in between the mast and the forestay. If the rat managed to get to the bag now, he was *Super Rat!*

In the end it took us a week of sleepless nights to catch him. Each day I moved the bread closer to the cage and then into the cage, but with the door open so he could get back out again.

Finally, we sprung the trap and wham, that night we had him!

In the morning, Chris went and had a look at him. He asked me whether I wanted a peek and I was pretty reluctant, but in the end my curiosity got the better of me.

I was expecting an ugly, disgusting, mangy beast, but Ben . . . (yep, he was Ben by now) . . . was a really young and handsome rat, as rats go, with sleek and healthy looking fur. And why shouldn't he be healthy? He had been very well looked after for at least a week!

Our friends had advised us to drown the rat in a bucket once we found it, but Chris and I were too soft for that. After all, poor old Ben had only done what comes naturally to rats; he had certainly not meant us any harm.

So, instead, we put the whole cage in a bag and took it ashore in the dinghy. We then went for a walk away from the Yacht Club until we found a patch of jungle. There we released him.

Our friends couldn't believe it!

Later, after we had left Brunei, we got an email from them, stating that "Our Ben" had showed up at the Yacht Club a week later.

I hope he got away!

CHAPTER 14

We left Brunei, minus Ben the Rat, and continued on our way down the northern coast of Borneo.

Here we faced another one of those unexpected challenges that keep the cruising sailor on his toes.

In the Pacific the main challenge was strong trade winds and reefs.

Going through Micronesia, there was the Counter Equatorial Current, running in the opposite direction to the prevailing winds, thereby causing rather large seas.

In the Philippines, there were the tidal currents to contend with. There were also hundreds of unlit small fishing boats at night. The fishermen are too poor to have proper navigation lights, so instead, they take along an old tin can or half a scooped-out coconut shell, filled with oil. When they feel threatened, they put a flame to it. I don't know if they are trying to save on the oil, but it seemed that generally they didn't feel threatened until we were just about to hit them. It was really frightening.

There you were, in the cockpit at night, peering into complete blackness. Sometimes, if it was a calm night, you could hear the fishermen chatting to one another, but you could not see them. On a couple of occasions I heard an outboard motor very, very close to us . . . but no lights. Then, just as you have convinced yourself that there is no one about . . . the click of a lighter . . . and on comes a light just about under your bows!

Philippine waters also provided another, even worse form of entertainment at night . . . the FADs. This stands for fish attraction device, and is a rather large and very solid metal buoy, completely unlit and placed in the middle of a navigable channel. Their purpose is to help the fishermen increase their catch, as the buoy usually attracts a colony of marine life around it.

Great for the fishermen! Not wonderful for us! It was pure luck that we did not hit one. We came very close a couple of times.

Off Borneo, we had been told there would be a lack of wind and oil rigs to look out for.

No problem. We thought we could handle that. At least the oil rigs would be lit. And hey . . . no wind . . . we'll just have to motor!

But...(there's that persistent "but" again) no one had spoken to us about the logs! Well . . . not quite true. I do remember a yacht coming in to the boatyard in Kudat with a bent propeller shaft. He had hit a log. We thought it was probably a rare thing. Hmmmm!

The logs off the coast of northern Borneo are a real hazard to a small boat. We are not talking about twigs here . . . We are talking about very large tree trunks . . . some were five metres long and more than a meter in diameter. They drift with the currents, so tend to congregate into huge debris fields sometimes several miles wide, and they seem to be everywhere. We thought if we'd stay well offshore we could avoid them, to no avail. Some of them were miles from the coast.

"Where do they come from?" you ask.

As far as we could tell, they were the result of the intense logging being carried out, partially to harvest the valuable hardwood, but also to clear the land for palm oil plantations. Now, normally you would have thought that the logging operators would have done their best to prevent the valuable logs from escaping, but I guess some escape when they are being floated down the rivers. Perhaps the big trees we saw were flawed in some way. Certainly there was a lot of smaller debris too, probably not worth harvesting. Whatever the reason, there is a fortune in wood floating about off the coast of Borneo.

For us, this meant doing our utmost to sail only during daylight hours. Even then, one of us was permanently sat on the forward hatch in the bows, peering ahead, to spot any logs. The debris fields were quite easily seen from a distance, but not so individual logs making a bid for freedom. The bastards seemed to do their best to remain undetected, waterlogged as they were and floating with most of their bulk underwater.

It was hard going and tiring. Both of us had to be on watch, one as a spotter on the bow and the other in the cockpit, ready to stop the propeller at short notice, to prevent it from being damaged if we hit a log. Even so, we hit quite a few. Fortunately the only damage was bits of paint being knocked off.

But worse was to come. There was one stretch of coast that really had no shelter for a night-time stop. So we were forced to try an overnight passage.

Once it got dark, there was, of course, no way at all to see the logs. We tried using a searchlight, but it hardly penetrated the gloom for more than a few metres in front of the boat. We could only hope that we would be lucky.

Bong! There was the first one. "Quickly! Turn the throttle to neutral!"

We shone the torch toward the scraping sound as the log bounced its way past us.

Silence for half an hour.

"Maybe that was the only one?!"

Bong! . . . same procedure . . . throttle to neutral.

"Bugger! That was a big one!"

Bong! This time the boat came to a full stop.

"What now?!"

The searchlight revealed that we had a huge tree underneath us, with a couple of meters sticking out on either side of the boat. We had hit it square on and *Skylark* had ridden up onto the log and stopped when it reached her keel.

We put the boat into reverse and backed off. We winced, knowing that this time there was sure to be some kind of damage. Thank God, the boat is aluminium. We would have a dent, but a boat of another material would easily have been holed.

The searchlight had also revealed that this was not an isolated log. We were in a debris field. How large was hard to tell, but we were certainly surrounded by logs. We decided it would be folly to try to carry on motoring.

There was only the slightest of breezes, not really enough to sail by, but we turned off the motor and raised the sails nonetheless. We spent the rest of the night ghosting along at one or two knots, all the while listening to the scrapes and bangs as logs and branches caressed our boat.

Dawn revealed the debris field that we had tried to motor through. It was enormous!

However, we did finally get to the Santubong River, our paintjob a bit worse for wear but propeller and shaft undamaged.

This was our stopping-off point before crossing the South China Sea to the Tioman Islands and then Singapore. It was also our first river anchorage, so new skills had to be put into play.

The trick here was to put down your anchor as close to the shore as possible because you wanted to avoid the middle of the river. Huge barges and rafts of floating logs would be coming down the river, and at least on *Skylark*, "log" was a bad word by then. On the other hand, there was a five meter tidal range, so you did not want to go so close to the shore that you would find yourself high and dry at low tide.

Tricky! Add to that the warning by cruisers who had been there before.

They had told us "Try not to foul your anchor. There are bits of sunken equipment on the bottom, just waiting to snag an unsuspecting anchor. Not nice to have to go diving here . . . There are crocodiles!"

We did our best and just prayed we'd be lucky.

It was worth a stop though. The nearby town of Kuching is a must-see. This place was once ruled by a white sultan . . . a British adventurer who was given the area to rule as his own kingdom, as a thank you for services rendered. That's the stuff of legends, isn't it?

In any case, we soon left the crocodiles behind . . . The anchor came up easily . . . thank God, and we had avoided being nipped in the bum by a reptile while getting ashore in the inflatable dinghy.

We headed off across the notorious South China Sea.

I remember a friend and yacht owner in New Zealand saying to us before we set off that he would never cruise further than the Pacific, because he wanted nothing to do with the South China Sea.

The place is famous for piracy of course, but it also has a reputation for fierce wind and waves. It is a shallow sea, so any heavy weather will tend to pile up the waves. As for the piracy, well, the South China Sea is surrounded by pretty poor countries, and that does tend to encourage piracy. In addition to that, a lot of the small island groups are disputed territory, making the locals rather trigger happy and hostile to visitors.

We had such an island group, the Anambas Islands, right on our path, and it would have made a convenient overnight anchorage, but caution being the better part of valour, we decided against it, unless we encountered very strong wind and needed to shelter there.

As it was, we were incredibly lucky. The fierce South China Sea was on its very best behaviour for our crossing. It was glossy, flat calm. We had to motor all the way. So calm, in fact, that poisonous sea snakes were taking the opportunity to rise to the surface and do a bit of sun bathing! Never seen that before, or since, for that matter!

We reached the Tioman Islands in three days. These are islands off the south-eastern coast of Malaysia and we had been recommended to stop there.

They were indeed lovely, and the clear water a contrast to the murky coast of Borneo. For the first time in ages we were able to snorkel and swim to our hearts' content. We were also able to check the hull of the boat for log damage, and were pleased to see that it was no worse than a few large patches of missing paint.

The islands were small and pretty, with white sand beaches. Sadly, the beaches were strewn with rubbish. The South China Sea is full of it. Even miles out at sea we would see plastic bags every couple of meters or so. Apparently, the locals sweep the beaches in the tourist season. However, we were there off-season, and the beach sweepers were on their annual break.

This was the season for heavy weather off the East Coast of Malaysia, so we did not linger long. We girded up our loins for the approach to the Singapore Strait, one of the busiest waterways in the world.

CHAPTER 15

We approached the Singapore Strait with great caution. Luckily, because we had sailed up to the Tioman Islands, we were already on the shore side of the Straits so did not have to cross the shipping lanes.

That is the greatest challenge in places like this. Imagine trying to cross a busy highway while on foot. It's a bit like that. Sure . . . the big ships are nowhere near as fast as a car, but they are a hell of a lot faster than a small sailboat. They also cannot manoeuvre much in a restricted space like the Straits. So, you have a line of giants to play dodgem with.

It's counterintuitive. You spend your sailing life trying to stay as far away from big ships as possible. Now you actually have to aim for them. The idea is to be as close as possible, when one passes you, so you can nip over the shipping lane right behind their bum, before the next behemoth is upon you. Heart-stopping stuff!!!

Luckily, in this instance, we were already on the correct side. But we still had to make our way through the anchorages. There were literally hundreds of huge ships at anchor everywhere. They are no threat while they are anchored, but at any given time, some are coming and going into the anchorage or engaged in anchoring manoeuvres . . . and you can get squashed if you are not careful. If you are close to them, they cannot see you.

Imagine being in a car and trying to avoid a mouse.

Oooops...sorry...little mouse...didn't see you there!

Nonetheless, we made it to the quarantine anchorage, where we were supposed to wait to be boarded by Customs.

This was a bit bizarre, as well. The quarantine anchorages are designed for big ships, not little boats. In consequence the area is very deep, much deeper than where small yachts usually anchor. We found a buoy, mounted on a rocky reef and approached it cautiously, looking for shallower water to anchor in. We succeeded in putting the anchor down, called Customs, gave them our position and sat down waiting to be boarded.

They obviously did not think we were very important. We watched the Customs boat approach ship after ship after ship, some of which had entered the anchorage way after we had. Had they forgotten about us? We called again and were told to wait.

It started to rain . . . torrentially, one of Singapore's famous thunderstorms.

Finally a small grey speedboat, with no markings on the side approached us. They then told us that they did not like where we had anchored. We must pull our anchor up and anchor where they were indicating. The spot they wanted us to re-anchor was about a hundred metres from where we had been.

"Why?" . . . Go figure!

Next, someone stood on the bows of the speedboat and shouted at us to hand over our passports. To our surprise, they were obviously not planning to come aboard . . . even though it was still raining very hard.

Chris was about to hand over the passports when I shouted at him to stop! I had visions of our passports getting wet in the rain, or worse, getting dropped into the water, as the speedboat was still keeping a distance between us and it. I quickly fetched a wet-bag and put the passports inside. The speedboat approached, took the wet-bag and left.

It now occurred to me that we had just handed over our passports to people in an unmarked speedboat. We had no way of knowing whether they really were Customs! We just assumed.

Anyway, they eventually returned, asking for more papers. All had to be handed over to the guy on their bows, over a gap of water. I was not happy! Why on earth couldn't they just send an officer over onto our boat? They boarded all the ships!

Who knows? All I can say is that Singapore obviously is not set up as an entry port for yachts.

We had the same trouble leaving there. Customs made us wait for more than two hours in the anchorage while they boarded ship after ship after ship. This time they even told us we were not a priority for them.

We pleaded with them not to delay, as the tides in the Straits produce a very strong flow and we would not be able to motor against it. We had carefully planned the timing of our departure for a favourable tide and they almost forced us to abort the departure due to the delay in processing us. They did not care . . . and told us so!

However, Customs aside, we did enjoy Singapore. Again I was struck by the enormous contrasts that you experience while cruising.

A week before, we had been anchored on a muddy, crocodile-infested river, surrounded by jungle. Now we were in a hyper-modern city, all chrome and glass and glossy high-rise buildings. Within an hour of arriving we had three new plastic cards to enable us to access marinas, ride the subway, and make a phone call.

We were lucky to also experience the gentler side of Singapore. A dear childhood friend, Kathy, lived there, with husband Steve and two children. They lived the privileged life of the Singapore expat: beautiful homes, luxurious clubs, Mah-jong afternoons, and cocktail parties.

It was approaching Christmas, and we had made arrangements to spend the holidays with my brother Ole and his wife, Rema, in Kuala Lumpur, further up the Malacca Strait.

So, we picked our time, dodged the ships, and headed up the Strait. We stayed just to the sides of the shipping lanes to avoid being run over. We also did not want to be too close to shore as we would then run the risk of running into one of the numerous fishing nets left unattended there.

Here was a new challenge . . . the fishing nets. These were to be an issue in our sailing for the entire time we spent in Malaysia and Thailand.

The local fishermen lay long nets, sometimes a hundred metres in length or even more. They are marked by a small flag on a pole at either end. The pole is often no more than a stick attached to a piece of Styrofoam, and the flag a bit of rag that used to be someone's clothes. In between these is a submerged net, though how deeply submerged is anyone's guess.

The trick is to spot the poles and then avoid sailing or motoring between them. If you are sailing it is not such a big problem. Unless the net gets caught in the keel or rudder, you can usually slide over them. However, winds in this area are fickle and you often find that you have to motor. What you want to avoid at all cost is getting the net entangled in your propeller. This results in a dive over the side with a knife to cut yourself free, and if you are unlucky, an angry fisherman clamouring for compensation.

I am not exaggerating when I say that these nets seemed to be everywhere. Just like in Borneo, with the logs, we had to have a spotter at all times, looking for the small flags that marked the nets.

The other phenomenon that makes navigating these waters a bit nerve-wracking is the thunderstorms. The area is called "Lightning Alley" by cruisers. There were magnificent thunderstorms pretty much on a daily basis. They would come upon you, seemingly out of nowhere, and apart from the thunder and lightning, they would be accompanied by strong winds, whipping the previously calm sea into a frenzy of waves.

The wind and waves were not so much of an issue. We were used to squalls, from our sailing in the Pacific. We just had to be alert and take down sails immediately if we saw one approach. It was the lightning that worried us the most.

It is not uncommon in this area, in fact it happens a lot, that yachts are hit by lightning. The results can be disastrous. Not so much for the people on board; they are usually okay. However, the accompanying magnetic pulse can destroy all the yacht's electronics, even things that were never connected, still in their Styrofoam packing. Apart from the inconvenience, we are talking about thousands of dollars worth of equipment which can be wiped out in one lightning strike.

Even worse, the strike can actually sink a boat. We saw this happening in an anchorage in Langkawi. The boat anchored next to us, a catamaran, was hit by lightning. There was a huge *BANG* and then a cloud of brown smoke enveloped the top of their mast. We saw the people on board emerge to check for damage, so we knew they were okay. However, later we heard that their bilge pump had started to go, and they quickly had to up-anchor and head for a boatyard to be hauled. The lightning had blown small holes in their hull!

In any case, though nerve-wracking, there is not much you can do to avoid a lightning strike. Some boats have lightning rods attached or drag chain behind the boat to allow the path of the electrical surge an easy exit. We are lucky that *Skylark* is aluminium, making us a sort of Faraday cage. We hope this will help . . . though . . . touch wood . . . the theory has never been tested.

We do wrap some emergency equipment, such as a handheld VHF and GPS and the back-up hard drive to the laptop, in aluminium foil and store them in our oven. This might help them survive a lightning strike. We don't have a microwave, but that is apparently the best place to store stuff to keep it safe from lightning. Microwave ovens are designed to keep microwaves in, so they work in the reverse as well and keep the microwaves out.

However, we were lucky, and neither fouled our prop in a fishing net, nor were hit by lightning in the Malacca Strait. Nor did we see either hide or hair of any pirates.

I think we were too busy worrying about nets and lightning to even worry about pirates. Besides, although there is still the occasional assault on ships in the Malacca Straits, we have heard that it has been awhile since a small boat has been approached. We were told the Straits are now quite well patrolled by the Malaysian Coast Guard.

Our experience, or should I say non-experience, with pirates up to that stage is an important point to note. We, and other boats like us, who had sailed through several notorious pirate areas successfully, were naturally starting to wonder what all the fuss was about. This whole pirate thing was starting to appear blown out of all proportion to us. All we had met were wonderful and friendly people. If we were ever approached by a boat, and that was rare, they turned out to be fishermen giving us a friendly wave or a warning that there were nets about.

Look at it this way . . . if you had walked through Central Park in New York safely for years, you would start to think it isn't as dangerous as some would have you think! Wouldn't you?

Whether right or wrong, I do believe that this kind of thinking had an impact on our decision-making later on. To our detriment!

CHAPTER 16

Many cruising boats treat the Malacca Strait as a thoroughfare on their way between Borneo and Thailand. The thunderstorms, nets, and piracy can certainly be a deterrent.

However, for those interested in history, there are treasures to be found here.

Those that head straight for Thailand often discover this area the second time around, if they decide to stay for more than a season. In comparison to Thailand, the Malaysian officials are so much more easygoing. In fact the whole country has a lovely attitude. People are friendly; you don't find the droves of tourists that you find in Thailand. You can walk down a street unmolested, and it's actually quite a bit cheaper to live in Malaysia. What you don't find is clear water, so generally snorkelling and diving are out. Instead, this cruising ground is all about local history and culture. Trading ships from all the cultures of the world have plied these waters for millennia.

We were fortunate in that we had a very good reason to stop here, so were never tempted to just pass through.

My brother Ole had married here and made it his home for the past twelve years. His wife, Rema, is an Indian Malaysian; that is Indian by culture, Malaysian by birth. That's one of the things that make Malaysia so interesting, so rich in culture. There are three main ethnic groups: the majority Muslim Malaysians and the minority Chinese Buddhist Malaysians and Indian Hindu Malaysians. Each group has added the special flair of their culture to the food, clothing, festivals, etc. It's a fascinating place.

Our plan was to spend Christmas there.

I come from a very small family. There is really only myself, my brother Ole, sister Pakeezah, who lives on the Isle of Wight, and Mum, who was at that time living in Mysore, India.

Mum had retired from the Swedish Foreign Office some ten years before and decided to live out the rest of her days in a nice warm climate, India.

Our family had always been geographically scattered, so opportunities to spend a Christmas together were few and far between. It had not happened in over a decade.

So, what with Chris and I passing through Malaysia on our yacht, my brother and sister-in-law living there and Mum not being all that far away in India, we decided to fly Mum over from India and celebrate together in a place called Port Dixon, conveniently close to Kuala Lumpur where there was a nice marina for us. The plan was for us to continue on to Thailand immediately following the holidays.

Remember how life had seemed to conspire to stop me from pursuing my cruising dream? I thought that I had successfully escaped its clutches by now. My health was holding its own; I had paid to have a CT scan done in Borneo and all seemed to be well.

But this time it wasn't my health that was the issue. It was my mother's. Neither my brother nor I had seen Mum in more than two years, pretty normal for our family. When we had last seen her, she was well; a little forgetful and eccentric perhaps, but generally fine. However, when she did not show up on her scheduled flight, we started to understand that something was wrong, very wrong.

It's a long and very sad story and I don't feel this is the place to tell it.

Suffice to say that life had struck in a big way. Mum had Alzheimer's, and quite advanced at that. When she finally did arrive in Malaysia, it was with the help of the Swedish Embassy and she was not going to be allowed back into India, as she had forgotten to renew her visas for the past few years. Sadly, she did not recognise either my brother or me and had no idea where she was. She was diminished in every way, physically and mentally; in fact she was really not my mother any more. She was a geriatric five year old, who held my hand and called me "mamma."

Logistically, we now had a big problem. The dream-stealers would have been happy.

Mum's dream had been to retire in India, and she had followed that dream. Unfortunately, this put her in a sort of no-man's-land where healthcare was concerned. She was a Swedish citizen and had paid taxes there all her life, but she had left Sweden voluntarily, emigrated in effect, and was no longer entitled to the otherwise very generous benefits of the Swedish healthcare system.

On the other hand, neither my brother nor I were in a position to provide her with the care she needed. With a bad hip, she couldn't even get on my floating home, let alone live there.

There was nothing for it . . . I would have to take her back to Sweden, and throw myself at the mercy of the authorities there. I myself had not lived in Sweden since I was nineteen and had no idea how things worked. Nevertheless it had to be done.

We knew it would all take quite a chunk of time, so we decided to try to make the best of things and purchased a one year marina contract in Port Dixon. Chris would stay there with the boat, while I did what I had to do. He would use the time to do repairs and maintenance, even haul the boat and repaint the hull.

I took my poor mother by the hand and took her to Sweden.

Neither of us had warm clothes. We arrived in Stockholm in cotton blouses and sandals in early February . . . the snow in droves outside.

What followed next was a really horrible and stressful period of my life. However, yet again, I was humbled by the help I got, especially from my aunt Barbara, not even a blood relative, but the recently widowed wife of my mother's brother. She stood at the airport with scarves, hats and boots to greet us. She herself was in deep mourning, but put her own feelings aside to help us through this awful situation.

In the end, we lost a year of our cruising.

That's a silly way to put it, isn't it? How do you lose a year?

Yes, we were delayed a year, but the year was not lost. Chris had done great things to the boat while I was gone. As for me, it was a year I wouldn't want to repeat, but at the end of it, my Mum was in a lovely, safe environment in a care home in Sweden, and I had gained something too. I had grown to really love my mother! We had never been very close, in fact, quite the opposite. However, in taking the role of her guardian, her protector, I had thoroughly forgiven her for any real or imagined wrongs she may have done to me in life, and found a real love in my heart for her, even as she was now, in her diminished state.

And . . . how much sweeter it all was . . . to be back on the boat.

We left Port Dixon in mid-November. My brother Ole was crew for the first leg, up to Penang.

On this stretch, we were able to do day-hops, a blessing . . . on account of the fishing nets.

It was a luxury to have my brother on board. An extra crew member made all the difference. We could look out for the fishing nets in rotation.

I think at this stage, we had ceased to worry about pirates in this area. There seemed to be a lot of yachts travelling up and down the Strait and we had not heard any stories of anyone being approached.

What we had heard, on the other hand, was that the marina in Georgetown, Penang, was a hazard. We were determined to stop there though, as we had also heard the town was one of the gems in this area.

As it turned out, the rumours about the marina were greatly

exaggerated. There were ferries passing close by, causing turbulence in the water. You had to expect your boat to roll around and needed to secure it carefully so as not to get your spreaders entangled with the spreaders of the boat next to you.

It's true, we did see a boat get damaged there, but we were okay. The greatest challenge was the very loud music from the nightclub adjacent to the marina. It was like having a disco on your foredeck till 3 in the morning every night.

But . . . it was worth it!

Penang remains one of my favourite Asian cities. It has managed to retain its character of a bustling Chinese/Indian trading centre, with shop-houses and gorgeous mansions, fantastically decorated, lining narrow alleys. Ancient temples vie for space with busy markets and there is a "Little India" where you could be excused for thinking you had been transported to that subcontinent.

And . . . Penang is famous for its food . . . in an amazing variety. It is truly cheaper to eat out than cook on the boat here. Who had eaten what . . . and where . . . was the main topic of conversation among the cruisers in Penang.

Last stop in Malaysia was the island of Langkawi, just on the border to Thailand.

This was a major cruising hangout. The island in itself is a lovely place, with some pretty bays to anchor in, and even some nice beaches.

However, the main attraction for the yachts seemed to be the safe and relatively inexpensive marinas. Thailand has a cruising season, outside of which you could be in danger of encountering a tropical storm. During the off-season therefore, you need to find shelter in a marina. Marinas in Thailand are becoming more and more expensive. Added to that, Thailand has awkward rules about leaving your boat in their country. You have to put large sums of money in bond in a local bank, if you plan to fly home for a month or two, leaving the boat there.

In Malaysia everything is easier and cheaper and even safer, as the Malacca Strait provides some shelter from tropical storms. So, many cruisers spend the off-season hunkered down in a marina in Langkawi, with an air conditioner attached to a hatch.

Having already been delayed for a year in getting to Thailand, we were anxious to carry on, so only planned a brief stop in Langkawi.

Again, life had other plans.

We met up with a good friend there, Steve, a fellow cruiser, whom we had last seen in New Zealand, some five years previously. He and his wife Gayla were cruising the world. Many years ago, when we were both in our twenties, Steve had been my boyfriend and we had sailed together for quite some miles.

On one of these adventures, he had fallen overboard, with me asleep down below, four hundred miles out at sea. If I had not woken up and managed to stop the boat, Steve would have died that day. His family, therefore, had always regarded me as somewhat of a guardian angel.

By a strange coincidence, here we were again, in the same place at a time when he was once more in need of a helping hand. He was on his way to Penang for tests which were to reveal that he had colon cancer and needed immediate surgery. His wife was unable to be by his side, as she was in the States attending to her sick mother. Instead, Steve and his family asked whether they could "borrow" me for a couple of weeks, to stand by him through this ordeal.

It was not hard to figure out what was the right thing to do . . . and of course we agreed.

Steve's wife later started calling my husband Chris "Saint Christopher." It is not every husband who sends his wife off to nurse a former boyfriend for two weeks.

So, yet again, I left Chris on *Skylark* and took a ferry to Penang.

Three weeks later, we were again on our way to that elusive place . . . Thailand.

CHAPTER 17

We were so excited! After more than a year of delays, we had finally reached Thailand.

Leaving Langkawi, you are literally within Thai waters in a couple of hours. There is a chain of islands, with many pretty anchorages to choose from. Officially, you are not supposed to anchor anywhere until you have cleared your boat in upon arrival in Phuket. However, unless you ignore all the islands in between and head out to sea for a couple of days, Phuket is still several day-hops away. A sort of unspoken compromise has developed over the years. As long as you don't dawdle too much, the Thai officials don't mind if your trip between Langkawi and Phuket takes a week or so.

Again I was struck by the wonderful contrasts provided by the cruising life. Ever since we had arrived in Borneo a couple of years previously, we had been sailing through murky water, with few islands, few beaches, and few snorkelling opportunities. Especially in the Malacca Strait, the water had been mostly murky brown, with the odd blue patch, and lousy visibility.

Two hours later, it was like being in the Pacific again. *Skylark* was once more transformed into a platform for water activities. I remember that first anchorage. How utterly delicious to jump into that warm, clear water again! How lovely to float about for hours just looking at coral and rainbow coloured fish! How incredibly lucky we were to be there! And the beaches had white sand again!

Palm trees, coconuts . . . and . . . what is that over there? . . . Oh . . . a sort of shrine . . . perhaps a Buddhist shrine? . . . No wait . . . it's not a Buddha . . . It's a penis . . . in fact many penises . . . Or is that penisi?

I kid you not . . . This was a Penis Shrine! There were penises carved out of wood . . . very lifelike . . . in all sorts of sizes. The largest one was about a metre long and a foot in diameter. Apparently the local fishermen set these up to increase their manhood . . . give them luck in fishing and make them more fertile.

Isn't life wonderful! How boring it would be if we were all the same!

After a week of gorgeous stops, we arrived in Phuket. We had been advised to avoid the main port and anchor in a bay on the West Coast of Phuket. From here we could take a taxi or a motorbike to complete formalities. So we headed into the southernmost of the bays that line the west shore of Phuket Island. And headed right into the "but" factor.

I know . . . you're starting to think that I am a bit of a drama queen, always looking for negatives.

Actually not true. I think I'm generally regarded as being pretty positive, as someone who always finds the silver lining. But I promised you an honest story . . . and that's what I intend to deliver.

We wanted so much to absolutely love cruising in Thailand. We had visited the country by plane before and it was one of our truly favourite places on the planet. Lovely people, laid back attitude, gorgeous food, great climate . . . What was not to love? We had dreamed about finding some remote spots, places still untouched by tourism . . . the real Thailand.

There are such places . . . but we were not to find them anywhere near Phuket. In short, the first landfall on Phuket was a bit of a shocker. The bay was pretty enough, and there was a beach. However, the beach was barely visible under the hundreds of beach chairs that lined the shore. Behind the beach chairs we could see one restaurant after another, interspersed with small shops touting souvenirs and local bric-a-brac.

Never mind, we thought. We have blundered onto a tourist trap. The next bay will be better.

The next bay was, if anything, worse. More tourists, more beach chairs, more restaurants, more everything. As soon as you stepped ashore, you were approached.

"Come into my shop!"

"Buy this T-shirt!"

"Want a massage?"

"Eat here!"

"Taxi?"

In one shop we saw a T-shirt that summed it up: *"No! I don't want a f...ing massage, nor a T-shirt, nor a beach chair!"* You get the drift.

Worse for us was that we did not even find sanctuary from it all at anchor. Every bay seemed to have a jet-ski rental. It was obviously great sport to "buzz" the yachts. Overhead, the dangling legs of tourists hanging under a parachute towed by a speed boat. It was anything but tranquil.

We did not say much to one another about it at first; didn't want to voice our disappointment. We had so been looking forward to this place. Surely it would get better.

I decided that I was not going to let the place be spoiled for me by getting irritated by the tourists. I decided that generosity was required. I was so incredibly lucky, living on a boat. Warm places, lovely water, exotic food; these were part of my everyday life . . . I could have them any day of the week. These poor land-based tourists, however, they came from cold places. They lived in Russia, Sweden, Germany. Their lives were based in the cold and the gloom. Once a year they would get to spend a couple of weeks in my paradise. Who was I to deny them that?

No, I thought. I could share. I would be generous and share my paradise with them . . . be happy for them . . . not be irritated by them. I tried to think this way, whenever the tourist trap got to me. It worked . . . sometimes.

Fortunately things did get better. We finally found a bay, at the very north-western tip of Phuket, which was not quite so touristy. There were a few hotels and restaurants, but no jet-skis. We hung out there for a while and loved it.

While there, we received a visitor from the UK, a friend, David, who owns a small yacht in the Solent and had invited us to sail with him many times. It was David's first experience of tropical sailing and we wanted to show him the very best of cruising life. So we decided to head away from the tourist trap in Phuket and see what we could find further up the coast of Thailand. The plan was to day-hop along the coast northward and then head offshore to some reputedly lovely islands called the Surin and Similan Islands. It was while on the way up the coast that we had one of those unique being-in-the-right-place-at-the-perfect-time experiences!

At one point the coast was bordered by several large barrier islands and it was possible to go in behind them, where there was a narrow channel through mangroves, almost an inland waterway. It was a bit nerve-wracking, as the channel was shallow and the water a murky brown. We did not have much info on the area, except that we had heard from other cruisers that one could come this way.

It was a bit adventurous for Chris and me really; we are known for being pretty cautious. Probably showing off a bit! . . . We did, after all, have a guest on board who was an experienced skipper in his own right . . . and we were supposed to be the world cruisers . . . One has to stretch a bit . . . if you know what I mean. Ha!

Anyway, all was going well, when we came upon a little fishing village. It looked absolutely idyllic. There were bamboo thatch huts on stilts overhanging a white pristine beach. Local fishing craft were pulled up on the beach. There was neither a tourist boat nor yacht in sight.

Photo opportunity! We decided to stop . . . on some flimsy excuse . . .

"We are out of biscuits" I said . . . "Perhaps there is a small shop?"

We motored gently toward the village to find a good anchoring spot. All of a sudden, out of nowhere, a small speedboat approached us. It looked pretty official; the guys on board were wearing uniform.

Now what?

They had no English and our Thai was pretty much non-existent, but they seemed to be indicating that we could not move about in this area. We either had to move on out of there or anchor. So, we anchored and indicated that we wanted to go ashore.

Nope! Not possible! They were saying something about "The King of Thailand."

They pointed around them, and for the first time we noticed that there were a large number of official-looking vessels moving about. We also noticed, on closer inspection through binoculars, that the village was festooned in brightly coloured banners and flags. Something exciting was definitely about to happen here! We guessed it was an official visit of some sort, but were confused as to why a small insignificant fishing village should be the venue of something of obvious importance.

Anyway, our officials in the speedboat seemed pretty happy with us at anchor as long as we did not move about in the area. They had communicated that it would all be over in a few hours, and then we could go ashore.

Fair enough! We were pretty excited to get to see what we thought would be a royal yacht; maybe even a glimpse of the King. In Thailand, the royal family is incredibly popular, in fact, revered. Whatever you do, you must never say anything against the royals. It is even considered offensive to drop a banknote, as the King's image is on it.

Well, we waited for hours, binoculars at the ready. Nothing happened! No royal yacht, no King. There was just a bunch of officials in various vessels moving about.

By late afternoon, our friendly officials told us "Okay . . . can go village!"

So we did. On shore we were able to find someone who spoke a little English. They explained to us that, indeed, there would be a royal visit, but it was to be tomorrow, and it was the Crown

Princess, not the King who would be coming. It turned out that she was the patron of a charity that awarded prizes to villages that had been devastated in the 2004 tsunami. The village had to show that they had recovered well and done their best to help restore the marine life near them. For instance, this village had saved some turtles and were farming them and releasing them, to help restore the population. All the to-ing and fro-ing of officials had been the dress rehearsal for tomorrow's event.

There was tremendous excitement in anticipation of the next day's visit. Everyone had sprinkled fresh sand around their huts; there were food stalls set up with women preparing local specialties. The school was being decorated, and there were flags and bunting everywhere. For these villagers, it was obviously a once-in-a-lifetime event. We couldn't help but catch the buzz.

So . . . we decided to stay. We were told that would be all right, as long as we did not move about in the water while the Princess was there. If we wanted to come ashore we would need to do so early in the day and then would not be permitted to return to our boat until after the royal visit.

Fair enough! We went back to *Skylark* and decided to decorate the boat by "dressing overall," that is, flying all our signal flags from the mast.

By early the next morning, activity was building to a crescendo. Typical Thai long-tailed boats started arriving in droves, all packed with people from outlying villages here for the day, and all wearing bright orange T-shirts. Soon the beach was lined with boats. We took a backpack with some water and sandwiches, hats and cameras, and took ourselves ashore in the dinghy. We were still the only non-Thais there.

It was so wonderful! Here was the "Real Thing." We felt so privileged to be able to participate.

We wondered about the orange T-shirts. Everyone was wearing them. At one point I was chatting to a woman in a navy uniform, who spoke quite good English. She told me that orange was the Princess' birth colour and the T-shirts had the logo of the charity that she was a patron of. I asked if we could buy one, but was told that they were not for sale.

"However...come with me!" she said.

We were taken to a thatch hut and given a T-shirt each.

"Our gift to you!"

Now we could blend into the crowd. Yeah right!

It was a long, sweaty wait, in fact hours of waiting. But all the villagers were waiting too, so we all just made the best of it. People were very curious about us and we did our best to hold conversations in sign language, with the odd English or Thai word thrown in. It's funny how a thing like language doesn't really matter. We managed to communicate somehow, and we shared this long day with them all, unified in our stoic tolerance of the heat and the wait.

Finally, she came!

I guess I had been expecting a tiara and gown . . . silly me.

The Princess was wearing jeans and (you guessed it) an orange T-shirt. However, she was undoubtedly a royal. She just had that bearing. She was beautiful, young and beautiful, with her hair swept back into a long braid. A bearer held a very large parasol over her head at all times and when she passed, we all had to cower, heads down and seated on the ground. It was not even permitted to sit on a tree root. We had to be lower than the Princess.

She stopped here and there and chatted with the locals, who were obviously deeply in awe of her. After visiting the school, where the official ceremony was held, she stopped at each food stall to chat with the local ladies who had prepared the region's specialities. She herself did not taste the food but graciously offered it around to her entourage. And then she returned to her boat and was gone!

Just like a royal visit anywhere I guess. Hours of waiting for a brief glimpse.

But this was not about the Princess for us. We had a marvellous day, just being a part of that crowd. We had been given a rare glimpse of the real Thailand.

To top off the day, we were offered some of the food from the food stalls. One particular dish looked intriguing. There were opaque white circular bits in a peppery sauce. I asked the lady if it was *pla*, the Thai word for fish, She indicated "Yes" so I took a hearty bite of it.

Delicious!

Later, however, I was to see these same opaque white tube-like bits in a market. I had eaten a couple of nice fat grubs. Oh, well!

We moved on to the Surin and Similan Islands, and the advice we had been given was correct. They were definitely worth a visit. They are part of a national park and there was a fee to pay. But the water was crystal clear and the fish so friendly that you felt that you were on a first name basis with them in very short order. The tourist boats did venture here, even though it was 60 miles off the coast. But in the mornings and late afternoons the droves were gone, and we and the few other yachts there had that paradise to ourselves.

In the end, Thailand turned out to be just like most such busy tourist places. You just have to know where to go.

And there were even quiet anchorages near Phuket . . . on the eastern side. Here there is a large bay dotted with small islands. They are very dramatic, with cliffs soaring out of the sea to impressive heights. The price you pay for the lack of tourism here is that the water is murky, and there are not really any beaches to speak of. However, the area is a haven for local fishermen, and they will sell you fresh prawns straight out of their boats and into your frying pan. *Yum!*

If you spend some time in a cruising area, you tend to choose a bay or marina to be your home base. In Thailand we found a lovely bay not far from Phuket which we nicknamed "Expat Bay."

We kind of stumbled upon this place. At first sight, the bay did not look like an attractive anchoring area, as there was a large pearl farm, with accompanying nets and buoys stretched right across the bay. However, on closer inspection, it was possible to anchor between the farm and the shore.

The bonus was to be found on shore. There was a beach bar there called *The Ship Inn* which turned out to be a hangout for expats, Brits and Dutchmen mostly, who had made Thailand their permanent home.

Outside the bar, there was a palm tree. Nailed to the palm tree, going all the way up the trunk, were old flip-flops, sneakers, and beach shoes. A sign read "The Tree of Lost Soles."

Magic! I thought, and liked the place right away.

We made many friends here, and used the place as our home away from home. It was a refuge from the hustle and bustle of the tourist scene.

CHAPTER 18

And so, a season in Thailand passed quickly.

Ever since we got to this area, in the back of our minds . . . there was a small seed of fear . . . growing. We had now reached a point in our cruising where we knew that there would be some tough decisions to make. Eventually, we would need to move on, and from here, neither of our options were at all attractive. They were downright scary . . . and we were tempted to delay having to make a decision.

I think this happens to a lot of cruisers. Pretty much wherever you have started your journey, eventually, by following the winds and currents westward, most cruisers end up in Thailand. Because the journey onward from here is a tough one, whichever way you choose, and because Thailand is essentially a lovely place to be, people get stuck here. They choose to delay their decision and spend season after season see-sawing between Thailand in the summer and Langkawi in the winter. For some, it is the end of their journey. They choose to sell their boat rather than brave the alternatives.

Because from here there were basically two undesirable options to choose from.

Head across the pirate-infested waters of the Indian Ocean and into the strong winds of the Red Sea. Then traverse the Suez Canal and end up in the Mediterranean.

Cross the Indian Ocean in a more southerly direction. Go to the Seychelles, Madagascar, or Reunion and Mauritius, and then face the Cape of Good Hope with notoriously strong gales and currents.

Neither sounded like much fun to us. Pirates or storms? The second option would add at least two years to our journey toward the Mediterranean, and we were frightened of those southerly gales, which had claimed many small boats. The first option was a much faster solution, but there were those Somali pirates to deal with.

It was certainly tempting to just stay in Thailand. However, for us, there had always been an issue which coloured our decision-making: my cancer. When I got secondary cancer, they had told me that I would only have a twenty-five percent chance of surviving five years. At that time, Chris had sat me down and asked me what I wanted to do with those five years. There was no question that I wanted to go cruising . . . but where did I want to cruise? It did not look, at that time, like there would be years and years to dawdle about, as we had hoped. Decisions had to be made.

My decision at that time was that more than any other place, I wanted to sail in the eastern Mediterranean. I am a real history buff, and had always been fascinated with this part of the world. Greece, Turkey, Italy . . . so much had happened historically in this area, and I really, really wanted to potter about there.

So initially we had decided to hightail it to the Med, just passing through the Pacific and South East Asia. But this was not how it turned out.

I soon realised, after we had set off, that it was all good . . . all wonderful. I could be just as happy cruising in the Pacific as I could be in the Med. The place did not matter so much. As long as I had Chris and *Skylark*, I was happy to not rush through things, to take my time. If I did not make it to the Med, so be it.

Now, some years had passed, and against all odds, I seemed to be thriving. Perhaps I would be one of the lucky ones? Perhaps I would be spared?

But still . . . now that we were in Thailand, the Mediterranean started to exert a pull on me. The alternative of spending several seasons in Thailand, or even ending our cruising career there, did not appeal.

For other reasons too, our need to reach the Mediterranean had grown stronger. Chris' father was requiring a lot of care, a burden shouldered mainly by his sister, and we wanted to help. I wanted to be able to regularly visit my Mum in Sweden. The pattern that we had developed of flying home for a few months each year was stretching our finances to the max. We needed to be closer to home. Possibly we might need to come out of retirement for a while to bolster our cruising kitty. We needed to be in a place where it was possible to work.

Another factor was to be influential in our decision-making.

When we had first arrived in Langkawi, several months prior, we had once more bumped into our dear friends Fatty and Carolyn on *Wild Card*. They were just leaving Langkawi and heading for a couple of months in Thailand. And then they were going to move on. They had also agonized over which way to go. They had already taken the South African route on an earlier circumnavigation, and knew how rough those waters could be. In fact, their stories of the wild sleigh ride that they had experienced while approaching Madagascar had sounded terrifying to us.

Anyway, they were still undecided as they left Langkawi. They were leaning toward trying their luck with the pirates, but Fatty said that he would leave the decision until the very last moment. They would sail to the Maldives and then decide which way to turn. He said he was willing to risk his own neck, but he agonized over exposing his wife to the dangers of a hostage situation.

Anyway, they left, and we extracted a promise to keep us up-to-date with their journey, whatever their decision.

In the end they joined a super-convoy and attempted the Indian Ocean/Red Sea route.

While floating about Thailand that year, we followed their progress with bated breath.

Eventually they made it to Turkey.

Their comment to us was "Desi and Chris . . . You can do it!"

Certainly I am not implying that they made the decision for us; it was ours to make. But their input was definitely a factor.

As it would turn out, bad though it was, they had crossed through the pirates in 2010. During the months that followed, the piracy scene exploded; it got much, much worse. But, we did not know that . . . and to our peril . . . based our decisions on old information.

What we had heard, though, was that the Somali pirates were now also in the Seychelles and Madagascar, so we could add pirate danger to the South Africa option, making it even less attractive.

We were not the only ones agonizing about all this. It was pretty much a topic of conversation whenever we got together with other cruisers.

I can't emphasise this enough. No one . . . absolutely no one . . . makes a decision to sail through pirate-infested waters lightly.

Sometimes, when a yacht is captured, the press seems to portray the victims of the capture as irresponsible people larking about, sightseeing in a place in the world where they have no business being. This could not be further from the truth. I don't know of one single example of a yacht being out there . . . for fun. Some people may make the decision to go with a minimum of information. Some people may feel that the dangers are exaggerated. Remember . . . that most of us had encountered pirate-danger-areas before, and found them to be not as bad as portrayed. So possibly there was a tendency to downplay the danger. But, no one was out there being a tourist!

Some were simply on their way home. Some had made a commitment to circumnavigate, and thus had to carry on. Some were simply outraged that these pirates were taking away from us the basic freedom, as citizens of the world, to sail in whatever area we chose. For all of us, this was a bottleneck to get through as best we could . . . The alternative was to allow the pirates to kill our dreams, our chosen lifestyle. For many of us, our boat is not a plaything . . . It is our home, and for some it is everything they own. The prospect of having to sell up . . . because they were afraid to go on . . . was unthinkable.

In any case we had to make a decision, and at the time, the better choice seemed to us to join a super-convoy and try our luck with the Somali pirates and the Red Sea.

At the time that we made our decision, the prevailing knowledge, coming from sailors who had done this passage in the previous year, was that the danger was relatively low, as no yachts had been taken on that route for at least a couple of years.

The Chandlers, an English couple who were held captive for a year, were taken near the Seychelles.

The word was that the Somali pirates, though increasingly more organised, were targeting large merchant ships, not small yachts. The main danger was the "gauntlet," a stretch of Yemeni coast between Salalah in Oman and Aden in Yemen. This stretch of coast runs quite close to Somalia and was considered the most dangerous area. It would take ten days to negotiate and was best done in convoy. No convoy had ever been attacked. So, we expected ten days of stress.

We thought we were up to that. We could do that.

Before we left, the Chandlers were released weary but unharmed on payment of a large ransom. All the signs seemed to point us in the direction of a decision to try the Red Sea route.

Decision made, we searched for a convoy and found one that was within our means.

The organiser, Phillip, was taking his wife, young baby daughter, and one crew on the trip. We met Phillip and liked what we saw. We also felt that, if he was taking his two year old daughter along, he must be fairly confident of the safety of the trip. The convoy would be thirty boats strong, several of the boats known to us.

We paid our admin fee and felt lucky to be included. We also took comfort in the fact that there were three independent convoys being organised as well as many individual boats which were getting together in groups of five or six boats. In other words, we were not the only ones who had made the decision to cross the Indian Ocean.

CHAPTER 19

It felt good to have finally made a decision. The dithering was over.

We now tried hard to forget any alternative route and just concentrate on what was ahead. We focused on the fact that the most terrifying bit was going to be a short stretch, Salalah to Aden, just roughly six hundred miles. Even in a large convoy, this should not take more than a week. Our chances felt pretty good. Among thirty boats, even if there was an attack, we would have to be unlucky to be the one caught. We had heard that your position in the convoy was determined by when you had signed up. Obviously all the boats would prefer to be somewhere in the middle. We fervently . . . and selfishly . . . hoped that we had signed on soon enough to get a "safe" position.

In our meeting with Phillip, the leader of the convoy, he had told us that the plan was for all the yachts to make their way to the beginning of the "gauntlet" in Salalah independently, either sailing in company with others or by themselves. Then we would form a convoy for the dangerous bit and later either continue in company through the Red Sea or split up. It was up to the individual skipper how much or how little support they wanted. Phillip did say from the beginning that he was planning to extend the convoy beyond the traditional "gauntlet," as the pirates were now also active in the southern parts of the Red Sea.

During this pre-departure time, we were hearing reports that the pirate activity had increased dramatically since last year. It made us a little nervous, but we were so set on going that we tended to ignore the "rumours."

I think our first inkling that this was going to be much worse than expected was when Fatty and Carolyn on *Wild Card*, who had done the trip the previous year, sent us a manuscript of their soon-to-be-published book, *Red Sea Run*, describing their passage.

It was a page-turner and a bit of an eye-opener and kept us awake for nights. They described not only the rigours of the "gauntlet." For them the danger had started earlier as they crossed the Indian Ocean. They told of anxious nights, sailing without running lights, radar reflector, and AIS, trying to be invisible and running the very real danger of bumping into another boat or ship which was also trying to be invisible. There was, apparently, as much danger of collision as there was of piracy. They were very happy for their radar, their only means of seeing in the dark.

We had no radar! We made a last minute decision to buy and install one.

It was a very hectic time for us, these weeks before departure. The boat was going to be put through quite an ordeal, and we needed to be sure that we were in as good a shape as possible.

Everything was checked and double-checked. We purchased a new mainsail. We had just repainted the bottom, so that was good. There was a lot of stocking up to do. We would not be able to expect to see a decent grocery store nor a chandlery for months. Chris agonized over what spares to bring. He is a worrier. We jokingly say he inherited it from his Mum who could "worry for England." He wanted to have spares for every possible thing that could fail on the boat, but you can only carry so much. Decisions had to be made. I was kept busy making sure we had enough canned goods, flour, pasta, rice, etc., etc.

And then I decided to give the dodger another protective lick of paint.

Our boat is aluminium, but a previous owner installed a plywood dodger (a kind of doghouse to protect you from the spray) over the companionway. It was a great installation and did keep us nice and dry. It had a little hatch in the roof of it, so you could shout things and hand things through it to the person that was on deck.

Anyway, I was busy sanding this, literally in the days prior to our departure from Langkawi to meet up with the convoy in Thailand. We were ready. We were set to go. I noticed that the area I was sanding close to the hatch felt kind of spongy.

Oh no!

We had wood-rot in the roof of the dodger.

I don't know . . . it sounds like a small thing now . . . but I guess we were already so keyed up for this trip . . . that it felt like a major disaster. We could have just left it, and it might have held for the trip, but we knew that we were facing heavy weather through the Red Sea, and we did not want a weakness to worry about. It was not just a matter of staying dry. This dodger provided support for our solar panels and also was the base for the boom-crutch; it was where our boom was stored when not in use. In fact, Chris had to crawl on it every time he took the mainsail down and wanted to zip up the mainsail cover.

Well, we had two weeks up our sleeve before the convoy meeting. So, we got out the saw and started cutting back the wet wood.

The rot had penetrated a long way. We had to cut more and

more back. The fault was in the installation of the hatch. The dodger roof was curved, so the hatch should have been mounted on a frame. Instead they had cut down into the curve to get a flat area to mount the hatch. Here, in the grooves, water had collected, causing the rot. We almost had to replace the whole dodger.

In the end, we managed to cut out a two foot square section and then plug it with three layers of marine plywood. The place curved in two directions, so it was a hell of a job to get it to fit. We had to build frames and use props.

Anyway, just another example of skills that you have to acquire when you are a cruiser. We were not carpenters, but you need to be able to jump in and try to help yourself. We also put in some strengthening beams on top, so the final product was a lot stronger than before. We decided to not reinstall the hatch, as this had obviously been a weakness in the design. I am proud to say that the repair is all but invisible . . . and we were very glad that we took care of it. We would have enough things to worry about on the upcoming trip!

So, we set off for Thailand and the preliminary convoy skippers meeting. Things were feeling pretty good.

At this meeting we met up with the other participants, and there were all sorts. They were just ordinary cruisers like us. Several nations were represented. There were skippers with crew and even families. Everyone was a little nervous, like us, but determined.

Amazing what comfort there is in being part of a group! It felt almost festive. Surely there would be safety in these numbers. It almost felt like we had exaggerated the dangers of the trip. It almost felt like we were part of a rally . . . like the one we had participated in from New Zealand to Tonga.

Mind you . . . I have to say that Phillip did not mince words. He did not give us the impression that what we were about to do was easy. In fact he spoke at length about what we could expect if we were taken hostage. He knew the Chandlers and others who had been captured. He warned us, that even if we were released, the horrors of that captivity would remain with us for the rest of our lives. It was no joke . . . It would change us forever.

On the other hand, he said that chances of capture were still relatively slim, if we were careful and stuck to the rules. It was a huge ocean out there. You could fit Europe easily into the Indian Ocean.

In any case we left that first meeting still feeling that we were up to this challenge. A date was set for another meeting prior to departure from Thailand and for a meeting in the Maldives, for those who planned an early departure. Some yachts wanted to cruise in the Andaman Islands or stop in Sri Lanka. That was fine . . . as long as we all got together again in the Maldives.

However, our anxiety did increase at the final meeting of the convoy in Thailand, when one of the participants, who had been plotting all recent piracy attacks, showed us his chart depicting the activity.

The Coalition forces, navy ships, and various special task forces who are trying to get to grips with the piracy problem publish reports of sightings of suspicious vessels and actual attacks. They recommend that all vessels give the incident areas at least a hundred miles clearance.

The chart shown to us had circles of a hundred miles radius drawn around each piracy incident. The circles overlapped and covered the whole area which we were about to traverse! There was nowhere to go across the Indian Ocean that wasn't considered a "No-Go-Area."

The attacks had reached unprecedented levels with two or three attacks daily. The pirates had gone from being small unequipped groups in small boats with a captured fishing boat as a mother ship, to well equipped, highly organised groups, backed by the millions collected in ransoms. They were now using captured container ships as mother ships and attacking with not only machine guns, but with heavy weapons such as rocket-propelled grenades. The targeted merchant ships were responding by hiring mercenary soldiers as "security teams" to help them get through the area. It was a war zone out there!

But still we decided to go.

I guess the feeling was that Okay, that's all pretty awful for the merchant ships, but yachts are not targeted. It has nothing to do with us. Why would they want a yacht when they can attack a big ship and hold twenty crew hostage and squeeze money out of the insurance companies?

Phillip recommended that we take extra precautions by taking a much longer route, skirting the outside of the Indian Ocean, never far from land.

This would involve many extra miles as we would have to go north along the Indian coast for a bit. We would then cross at a latitude higher than any reported activity (at that time around 20° north) and later make our way down the Omani coast (considered safe) to Salalah, where we would convoy formally for the most dangerous part. This was a major change in plans and involved all sorts of difficulty, extra miles, and extra time, but it still seemed feasible. We also agreed that we would meet in the Maldives and, for safety, travel the Indian Ocean part in larger groups.

This sounded like a good plan to us. We were prepared to do the extra miles, if it was safer.

At this point, I guess we should have been wise and delayed until we got visas for India. However, we were on the eve of departure. Getting visas would involve a trip back to Penang in Malaysia and possibly an undefined waiting period.

We calculated that we should just manage the coast of India without stopping, if we took extra diesel on deck. And . . . we would be able to sail part of the way . . . after all.

It felt far scarier to get left behind . . . to watch the convoy sail off and leave us. We did not know if we would be able to pluck up the courage again, if we had to delay another year. We were already in this . . . It had taken on a momentum of its own.

CHAPTER 20

So far...so good. We set off for the Maldives, a two week sail, in the company of another boat, not because of any danger, but for the pleasure of each other's company. The cruising guide books described crossing the Bay of Bengal at this time of year as some of the best cruising one could expect to have. However, as we have found previously, global warming seems to have thrown off all weather predictions, and we got more wind than we had counted on. Still, it all went well until just off the coast of Sri Lanka.

We were about a hundred miles due south of Sri Lanka when we started hearing some strange noises from our auto-helm. Chris investigated and came to the conclusion that we had developed a problem, potentially serious, with our hydraulic ram. This would affect both our ability to steer and would eliminate the use of the autopilot . . . unthinkable on this long a journey with only two persons on board. We knew that there would be no mechanical workshops or chandleries on the small Maldivian island we were headed for, in fact no help for any serious issue for a very long time, so reluctantly, we decided we had better divert to Galle, on the south coast of Sri Lanka, to sort this out. We still had a bit of time up our sleeve, as departure from the Maldives was scheduled some weeks away. Several other convoy boats had also decided to stop in Galle, including our leader Phillip and his boat *Serendipity*, which had gearbox issues.

So we said goodbye to our companion boat, as they continued on toward the Maldives. We instead pointed north, toward the coast. It was roughly a hundred miles away. We should be able to get there the following morning. Chris was worried that the ram problem could get worse if we used the autopilot, so we had no choice but to hand-steer.

"Well . . . so what?" I can hear you say! "Isn't an autopilot a luxury? Surely in days of old, boats and ships were hand-steered all the time!"

Well . . . that is true . . . but they usually had gangs of crew to take their turn at the wheel. The odd single-hander . . . like Joshua Slocum . . . who circumnavigated by himself a couple of hundred years ago . . . used to tie a rope around his tiller when he needed a break. You can do that with a tiller . . . if you have an extremely well-balanced boat. You can't usually do it with a wheel . . . especially a hydraulically operated wheel like ours.

So, there was nothing for it except to sit at the helm for hours on end. I could usually manage two hours in a stretch. But that meant two hours, literally chained to the wheel. No going and making yourself a nice cup of tea. No going to the toilet. It also meant that naps were restricted to two hours in a stretch. It was to be a long night!

To add to our misery, it was extremely windy, blowing twenty-five to thirty knots, forward of the beam with two to three metre waves. Not extreme conditions; just uncomfortable. As we approached the coast, we also started to notice that we were being swept westward by a current. This was hardly noticeable at first, but the closer we got to the coast, the stronger the current got. To compensate, we had to point the boat further and further eastward. This meant closer and closer to the wind. Eventually we got to the point that the boat was almost stalled. We could not get her to go where we needed her to go. The headwinds were too strong. Even with the motor turned on we were being swept westward.

We started to panic. It is so easily done, when you are tired. We were picturing ourselves being swept right past our destination, Galle, maybe even being swept right past Sri Lanka. Then what would we do?! It was horrifying. The more nervous we got, the less able we were to hold the boat on a steady course. The less steady the course, the less headway we made. A couple of times we backed the sail and had to make a full circle to get back on course. And all this on a pitch black night with the wind howling around our ears. Massive confusion! In the end, we decided that we had to risk turning on the autopilot. At least it would hold a steady course and allow us time to trim the sails properly.

I have read somewhere that ninety percent of the things we worry about never eventuate. We needn't have been so worried. The current that had given us such a headache actually reversed eventually, now sweeping us in the other direction. Dawn came too . . . as it usually does . . . and things seemed so much less frightening. As we got closer to the Coast, both the wind and the waves died down. We were almost serene by the time we approached the harbour.

The time in Galle was stressful in its own way. We were desperate not to get left behind, and therefore under time press. The hydraulic ram issue went from bad to worse as the locals destroyed our existing ram in trying to "fix" it. We were forced to acknowledge defeat and import a new ram from the USA. We were very afraid that it would not arrive in time, but it did.

While we were waiting for our ram in Sri Lanka, we met crews of other boats, outside of our convoy, who were also intending to cross. One of these people was an American lady called Phyllis, with whom we had a cup of tea and a chat about yachting in general. She was in the process of changing yachts, having finished crewing on one and on her way to join another yacht. Sadly, she was soon to lose her life at the hands of the pirates. We also met the skipper of Danish yacht *ING*, who was attacked and taken hostage to Somalia along with his family and crew, including three children. But, all of that was still in the future. If only all of us had had a crystal ball . . . !

In the meantime, what with our imported ram and *Serendipity's* repairs, which also took longer than expected, as well as unseasonably strong winds, the departure date from the Maldives was delayed by a few days. Unbeknown to us at the time, the delays, the absence of leadership in the Maldives, and the resulting anxiety among participants were going to be the death knell to our super-convoy. It all fell apart.

The majority of the convoy yachts had not stopped in Sri Lanka and were now awaiting the arrival of the rest of us, off a small atoll in the Maldives. There is nothing much to do there except socialise with other yachties. These get-togethers developed into daily meetings on shore with all convoy participants discussing the escalating piracy problems every morning.

Facts and rumours were rife, and as our leader Phillip was not there to offer guidance, it seems that things rapidly got out of hand. We were not there, so all of this is hearsay, but it seems that the anxiety level spiralled out of control.

Finally the stress got so great that some participants felt they could not wait for the rest of the convoy and had to make their own decisions on how to proceed. The end result was that several participants decided to give up, turn around, and sail back to Thailand. Others decided to head south for the Chagos Islands and South Africa, and yet others decided they would put their yacht on a freighter and have it transported to the Mediterranean. Some took off to make their own way across the Indian Ocean by a more direct route than the long one recommended.

Now, I don't mean to imply that it was some kind of mass hysteria that led these other skippers to their decisions. In hindsight, they were wiser than we were. Things were escalating, and the most recent knowledge that they received was painting a far worse picture than anyone had anticipated on leaving Thailand. I also don't think anyone later regretted the decisions they made not to continue, even though some of us did arrive safely. We went through real danger and real mental anguish out there, and if Chris and I had known then what we know now . . . we would have made a different decision.

In any case, the reality of our situation was that by the time we reached the Maldives (in plenty of time for the planned departure date) our super-convoy of thirty boats, still wishing to sail to the Red Sea by the long route, was reduced to six, including us!

In hindsight, this would have been a good time to reassess our options, and we did wonder if we should go on. As many as sixteen of the original thirty boats in our convoy had decided to freight their boats to Turkey. The problem was that the cost would be about US$30,000 for this option. We just did not have the money. So, for us the only options available were to return to Thailand (a two to three week sail against the wind), to try our luck with the wind and weather around the Cape of Good Hope, or to carry on.

Ultimately, if we decided to carry on, we still had a group of six yachts for company including the leader. Also, several of the other boats that had gone ahead were reported to be willing to wait for us on the other side to form the planned convoy through the "gauntlet." Surely, six yachts travelling together, staying very close to land, skirting the entire ocean, never going too close to the attack sites, etc. . . . surely we would be okay?!

In addition to this, our convoy leader Phillip, who had been tireless in lobbying the navy and anti-pirate Coalition forces to recognise our group of yachts and give us some protection, finally appeared to be getting some results. Though no one wanted to say that they could provide an escort, at least he was getting some calls back from people in power, and we hoped that we might have a chance at a warship hovering close by, at least for the most dangerous part of the crossing.

For better or for worse (gulp), we decided that we would continue.

The plan was to stay very close to the Indian coast all the way up to Karachi. The idea of going to Karachi was a new one. Yachts never go to Karachi. It was a complete unknown and not even in any of the cruising guides.

However, we had a not insignificant complication . . . availability of extra fuel. The problem was that our new route was much longer than initially planned. A lot of this route would require us to sail straight into the wind (if there was wind), perhaps forcing us to motor-sail or to motor due to lack of wind (if there was no wind). Both scenarios would use diesel. We would definitely need to refuel somewhere.

India was out, as they had very strict visa requirements and most of us did not have visas for India. Remember...there had initially been no plan to go to India. So, instead, Phillip had been in touch with the Karachi Yacht Club (a small dinghy sailing club) to see if we could stop there to refuel. Apparently, visas would not be required in Karachi. We all carefully looked at our fuel supplies and even got extra jerry cans of diesel to strap on the deck. We thought we could probably make it from the Maldives to Karachi before running out. Our boat has a capacity of four hundred litres. We had an extra hundred litres of diesel in jerry cans of the deck. Theoretically this should give us a thousand miles of motoring, but only in benign conditions. In heavy seas you use much more. And if you are zigzagging against the wind, you can double the distance you have to travel. Maldives to Karachi was about a thousand miles. We thought we could make it. After all, we were planning to do some sailing too!

Oh, the innocence of that statement, in hindsight. What we did not know yet, was that we might as well throw out all romantic notions of using only wind power. On this kind of a journey, when you are scared, when you want to get out of the area as quickly as possible, when you want to make sure that you are not left behind if other boats are faster, you turn that motor on and you keep it on and you run it at revs higher than you have used before. Diesel was an issue and would remain an issue for the whole of the trip.

In any case, we prepared as best we could, said goodbye to the boats remaining behind, took one last look at the beautiful and safe Maldivian Islands, and for better or for worse, set off into the danger zone.

CHAPTER 21

There were fourteen of us in six yachts, leaving the safety of the Maldives.

I have changed their names and the names of their boats to protect them . . . but they are an important part of the story . . . so I want to introduce you to them, if only to show you that we were a bunch of ordinary people out there. Not heroes, not reckless adventurers, not hippies, as some would imagine . . . just ordinary people, who had been, or still were, highly regarded professional people in their pre-cruising existence.

The largest was the lead boat, a really gorgeous classic yacht, *Serendipity*. Aboard was our leader, Phillip, with his beautiful wife Lena, baby daughter Isla, and a young American girl, Meg, who worked as crew. Phillip had sailed from Turkey through the Red Sea and the Indian Ocean three years before. At that time, he had also been part of a convoy, and was using expertise gained on that trip to help us along. Our convoy was a not-for-profit enterprise as opposed to the other two large convoys out there. We did pay a fee to cover admin costs, but it was small in comparison to the fee required by the other two convoys. Basically, Phillip explained that he needed to get his boat home to Europe and knew that others had the same need. So he volunteered to be the organiser and leader.

Next we had a British husband and wife team, Penny and Paul, both doctors, on board a shiny new, very fast, state-of-the-art yacht, *Bliss*. Paul was a retired surgeon, and his wife a general practitioner and they were circumnavigating, having started in Hong Kong where they had lived for many years.

Gerhardt from Germany, another doctor, was sailing his yacht *Leah* together with American crew Robert. Robert was a photographer and along for the ride. He was making his way around the world and had grasped at the opportunity of this adventure. Gerhardt was glad to have him, as his attempts at getting family or friends to crew for him on this dangerous journey had been met with a resounding *"No!"*

Two Austrian brothers, Franz and Hans, were retired Porsche mechanics and sailed on their racing yacht *Geliebte*. They were completing their two year circumnavigation. They were on the homeward stretch, unlike Penny and Paul, who were just beginning.

American registered yacht *Libertad* was home to South

Americans Lucia and her husband Juan, both in their early thirties. They too, were completing a circumnavigation, on their way back home, where a job was waiting for Lucia.

Finally, there were Chris and I on *Skylark II* . . . but . . . you already know all about us.

Very soon after leaving the Maldives, it became clear that it would be very difficult for all six yachts to stay within sight of each other. The yachts were very different in size and speed and *Bliss* and *Leah* soon shot ahead of the rest of the pack. *Geliebte* and *Serendipity* were also much faster than us. Only *Libertad* seemed to be a match for *Skylark* in size and speed and we soon agreed that we would stay close. Still, we had an expectation of the six boats at least staying together close enough to have radio contact via VHF.

On the second day, there was an urgent call from *Serendipity*, now behind us but not in sight. She reported that her gearbox was failing again. They had a severe oil leak. *Geliebte* (the two mechanics from Austria) was standing by them, to see if they could help. Even *Leah*, who was well ahead, turned around and sailed back to their position. *Libertad* and *Skylark* stopped and held position to see what would eventuate.

By the next morning, *Serendipity* was under tow behind the much smaller, but powerful *Geliebte*, who had agreed to tow them to the nearest large harbour, Cochin in India. None of the crew on either boat had visas for India, but were planning to invoke an emergency clause that allows any ship to seek safe harbour in an emergency. Phillip told the rest of us to carry on up to Karachi. He would catch up with us there.

Now we were four!

By the next morning, *Bliss* and *Leah* had left us in the dust. They were just too fast for *Libertad* and *Skylark*. It was not a question of them abandoning the rest of us. We had agreed to sail this part of the ocean independently, and they were just much faster boats. However, we established a ham radio schedule with *Bliss* and they also took on the task of contacting UKMTO daily on behalf of all of us, to give updates on our positions. The UKMTO (UK Maritime Trade Operations office in Dubai) was acting as the primary point of contact for merchant vessels and liaison with military forces in the Indian Ocean. They issued reports on pirate attacks and also wanted to be informed of our whereabouts. They had emphatically advised us not to sail through this area, but as we had not heeded that advice, they wanted to keep track of us. In any case, although we had almost daily contact with *Bliss*, we were not to see either them or *Leah* again until Muscat.

Now we were two!

Just the young South American couple and us. Two small boats in a sea of trouble. We had no choice but to carry on and to stay really close to one another. Neither crew fancied braving these waters alone. At the same time we realised that two small yachts in company were not going to scare off any pirates. We felt extremely vulnerable.

We decided that stealth was our best weapon. We would not carry any navigation lights at night, only a small white light encased in a black sock to make it dimmer, so that we could just see each other. We had already taken down our radar reflectors, to reduce the chance of being spotted by the pirates on radar. We turned off our AIS transmitter, which would normally alert ships of our presence. We would not speak on the VHF, the short wave radio that we normally use to communicate with other boats in close proximity. Those transmissions could easily be heard by the pirates. Instead we set up a signal to alert each other of the need to communicate. We would whistle into the VHF. This would prompt us to turn on our ham radio sets on a certain frequency and talk that way. Even so, we would be careful what we said. We would never mention a position or a route on the radio.

In short, we were trying to make the best of the vulnerable position that we suddenly found ourselves in. We had signed on to be in the company of thirty boats. Here we were, just two of us. How on earth had that happened?! We did consider turning back, but that would mean retracing our steps back to the Maldives on our own . . . and then what? Besides, would it be right for us to abandon Lucia and Juan? They would be even more vulnerable without us. For better or for worse . . . we felt we had no choice but to carry on. It was a sinking feeling. We did not even want to think about the many miles that lay before us.

It did not help matters that it turned out that Lucia and Juan were especially anxious. As mentioned, they come from South America where hostage-taking and kidnapping is a frequent occurrence. Becoming a hostage meant undergoing unbelievable humiliation, being raped and worse, and often losing your life. They had decided that they would rather die than be taken by the pirates. They, therefore, had no intention of being taken without a fight. They had a shotgun and a pistol on board and intended to use them.

This was counter to what Chris and I believed in, counter to all advice that we had been given on the subject. Nonetheless, we could not expect them to abandon their right to defend themselves for our sake. Juan told us that if we were under threat, we were to position *Skylark* next to *Libertad* but on the side away from the pirates, so he would have a clear line to shoot. We just prayed that it would not come to that.

A few days later, however, this almost became reality. It was a completely calm day with good visibility. From a long distance we watched a rusty, suspicious-looking vessel stop in our path. It was about the right size to be a pirate mother ship. There were no birds circling overhead, so it did not appear to be fishing. It was almost dead in the water, so was probably not a freighter on its way somewhere. It seemed to be waiting for us to approach. Gulp!

We went to battle stations. We crossed behind *Libertad's* stern so as to put them between us and the suspicious vessel. We then closed up on *Libertad* so that we were as close to them as possible. I saw Juan crawl through the cockpit holding his shotgun. Lucia had the pistol.

It was all kind of other-worldly. I felt like I was in a TV movie or something. This couldn't be real! This couldn't be us! I could feel the stress starting to cloud my thinking . . . so I dashed below to look at the list which I had put up for this very purpose. I had anticipated that my mind would go blank in the event of an attack, so I had put up an "Emergency Procedure – Pirate Attack" check list on the bulk-head. I started to follow the instructions on it.

First item on the list was for me to put on a pair of long trousers; I did not want to be caught in a Muslim country, for months on end, wearing shorts.

Next I wrote down our position, latitude and longitude, and gave the note to Chris at the helm, along with the handheld VHF, so he could call a Mayday. Then I turned on the ham radio and tuned it to the emergency frequency, so that I could also call a Mayday.

I took the EPIRB (emergency position indicating radio beacon) off its holder and prepared to set it off and hide it, so it could emit our position to the naval forces out there. We had decided to hide it in a large toiletry bag which I would try and place on the deck through one of the hatches. It has a blinking light on it, when set off . . . and we anticipated that the pirates would probably force us to turn it off, if they saw it after boarding. The idea was to allow it to emit a signal for as long as possible.

All this, while Chris was holding position about a metre away from *Libertad*. My heart was beating furiously! Our worst fears might be about to be realised. *Would we survive?!!*

It was all a storm in a teacup! Thank God! The rusty boat saw us getting close to each other and decided to back off. They were probably poor fishermen, hoping for a handout from the rich foreign boats. I am sure that the fishermen are also aware of the piracy situation and that they know that some boats are armed. They do not want to be mistaken for pirates. They are also scared.

That is the problem out there. Although most boats are just friendly locals, you cannot know. When the pirates come, they look just like a fishing boat. They approach and when they are on top of you, they pull out the Kalashnikovs. You never know when it can happen. You are on your guard twenty-four hours a day, scanning the horizon day and night. Every skiff in the day, every light at night . . . could be *the one*. It wears at your nerves until they are at breaking point. We found ourselves screaming at each other for the smallest thing; we were in tears; we were at the end of our rope. And we had miles and miles to go. There was no escape. We just had to endure it and carry on.

At least we had *Libertad*. We clung to each other and we clung to the thought that no yachts had been captured in that area.

CHAPTER 22

About five days into the trip, *Libertad* informed us that their water-maker had packed up and that they were running short of water. To make matters worse, the one tank they did have had been polluted by seawater. They also were worried about diesel as we had been motor-sailing into strong headwinds and used up quite a lot of diesel.

We debated what to do. None of us had visas for India and we knew officialdom in India can be troublesome. On the other hand, we had many miles ahead of us and lack of water was an issue, even if we could somehow share what we had on *Skylark*. Reluctantly, we made the decision to try a small port in India called Malpe and invoke the emergency clause. We hoped the officials in a small port would be sympathetic and just allow us water and fuel.

Decision made, we headed for shore. We had no proper paper charts for the area, or any kind of cruising guide. However, we did have our electronic charts, which we hoped would be accurate enough. The inlet leading to the harbour entrance was shallow, so *Skylark II* led the way. We have forward-looking sonar, so would hopefully see a reef or underwater obstruction in time to avoid it. We anchored in just three metres of water just off the harbour entrance and *Libertad* launched their dinghy. The plan was for me to stay on board and watch the boats while the other three took the jerry jugs ashore.

Almost right away, a police patrol boat approached *Skylark II*. They indicated that they wanted to come aboard. I tried to put them off in a friendly but firm manner, saying that I was alone, my husband was away, and I was afraid of letting a bunch of strange men onto my boat.

They insisted, so there was no choice. Three of them came aboard. However, they were friendly enough, and the leader spoke good English. I explained our plight. He was sympathetic, but also did query why we did not have visas. He was friendly one minute and official the next . . . so it was a fine thing . . . but I tried to keep it light, offering them a cup of coffee, etc. I just kept repeating that we had not planned a stop in India and this was an emergency stop, only to get fuel and water.

It seemed that they were more curious than anything else. This was exciting stuff for them. They even wanted to take photographs with me sitting next to them . . . something to show their family.

In the end they seemed satisfied with checking the passports and went away to try and intercept the dinghy and talk to the rest of the crew. Whew!

Overall the stop in Malpe was a success. The officials were very friendly and saw our visit as a break in the tedium of their jobs. They even organised transport into town to pick up a few groceries. They wrote down our passport numbers; that was all.

In fact Juan and Lucia were all for spending a night at anchor, before carrying on. Lord knows we could all have used a full night's sleep. At that point we would have given anything for a good night's rest. However, I vetoed the idea. I felt that we had been lucky and should not push our luck too far. The officials we had dealt with were obviously minor officials. I was afraid that if they reported the day's events to a superior, everything could change and they might come out and detain us. The others reluctantly saw the reason in this.

We left without incident . . . well, almost. In our haste to get ashore, we had not checked carefully on the state of the tide. We had anchored in three metres of water to get as close to the harbour entrance as possible. By the time we were ready to leave, the tide was out and the waves had increased. We touched bottom several times on the way out. Fortunately the bottom there was soft mud and sand, so no damage.

We headed back out to continue our progress north.

We were all a bit discouraged when we re-crossed our previous track, no further north than we had been two days ago. Our visit to Malpe had cost us!

And so, we continued northwards. The going was harder than ever, with strong winds on the nose. We were all getting very tired and coupled with the stress, our thinking and resolve got muddled. We were just really dismayed at the thought of possibly another two weeks of the same northward battle before we could reach Karachi.

Then the news came via ham radio that Karachi as a destination was out. Although landing there with no visa would have been possible, they were not set up for yachts and would charge us the same landing fees as a large ship, in our case about $450.

This meant that we would have to sail right past it and continue another four hundred miles across the northern Indian Ocean to Muscat in Oman. Depression descended on all of us. There seemed to be no end to this miserable trip.

Just goes to show, how we really were not thinking straight. In hindsight, what a trifling thing a fee of $450 seems! It would have meant rest, safety for a few days . . . and for us . . . we could have avoided that second refuelling stop in India.

Hindsight is . . . as they say . . . 20/20 vision. But . . . I'm getting ahead of myself again.

Somewhere in the midst of our gloom, Lucia and Juan attempted to come up with a solution. What if we were to change strategy? We were getting daily updates on pirate activity via ham radio from a friend in Thailand. The pirate attacks seemed to be concentrated into two groups. One group was centred in the northern Indian Ocean, with attacks between 19° and 22° north latitude. The second group was from around 17° north latitude and south of that. No one had attacked around the 18th latitude. Perhaps we could cross there. It would certainly save time and miles and might be worth the risk?!

In any case, while Lucia was plotting out a course with suggested waypoints, we tried to reconcile ourselves to this new strategy. We also contacted *Bliss*, the British couple who were by now several hundred miles ahead of us. We thought they might want to backtrack a little and join us on this crossing. They didn't, and later told me they had an uneasy night because they thought it was mad to attempt a crossing at this latitude, but did not want to let us down by not staying with the group. In the end they said no.

I have to admit that Chris and I really struggled with this new plan too. Phillip had been absolutely clear in his advice to not attempt a crossing any further south than the most northerly reported attack. This meant not crossing until we had reached at least 23°. This seemed like sensible advice.

However, Lucia and Juan had another issue. They were under some time-press to get home. This was all taking much longer than anticipated.

By now, we felt quite a lot of solidarity with *Libertad*. We were a team. So far we had been in this together. We were torn between not wanting to be parted from them, and a fear of engaging in what seemed like a far riskier strategy. Anyway, in the end we decided to risk it and were now heading a little further north with the intention of soon commencing the crossing at the 18th latitude.

The very next morning, we all got the news that American yacht *Quest*, with four Americans on board, had been captured *on the 18th latitude just a few miles from one of our intended waypoints!*

I remember we were all very quiet on the radio that day. We did not even have to discuss the rejection of our latest plan. We just kept plodding on northwards, now with the knowledge that our last fragile thread to a feeling of security had been severed. They were not just after merchant ships; they would take a yacht and had done so.

Four days later, Juan told us quietly, "They have killed them all."

It is hard to describe how we felt at that moment. For myself, my mind was full of images of the horror that must have played out on that yacht. There were questions too. What went wrong? Did they try to fight back? Was there a gun battle? Why did they kill them when the only gain for the Somali pirates was the money they could collect in ransom for live crewmembers?

We grieved for those people, part of our yachting community. (We later found out that Phyllis, whom we had met in Sri Lanka, was one of them.) We also knew that we had made a huge mistake in judgement, just as the people on *Quest* had. This was not a simple cat and mouse game between us and the pirates. We were risking not just our freedom but our very lives.

And there was nowhere to go. We couldn't just say "We've had enough now! We want to go home."

Going back meant sailing miles and miles on our own in unsafe waters as *Libertad* would probably not return with us. We were afraid to try to land on the Indian coast again, without visas. We had heard of boats being confiscated for less. We could not stop in Karachi.

Worse, all sorts of political conflict was breaking out in several of the countries on our intended route. Though we weren't getting much news from the outside world, one email from Phillip said we might not be able to land in Yemen or Eritrea and there was trouble in Egypt. We were trying to sail through the Middle East at the time of the Arab Spring!

The Arab Spring was a series of uprisings and demonstrations against government that affected large parts of the Arab world in late 2010 and early 2011. It started in Tunisia and swept through the Middle East. By late January, as we were leaving Thailand for the Maldives, the uprisings had spread to both Yemen and Egypt, two countries on our route. Events had steadily gotten worse since then. While we repaired our ram in Sri Lanka, thousands of Yemenis protested all over Yemen in a "Day of Rage" and in Egypt many violent clashes between demonstrators and government troops led to Cairo being described in the international media as a "war zone." While we were in the Maldives, Egyptian president Mubarak stepped down as president. While we were getting fuel in Malpe, Yemeni protestors declared a "Friday of Anger."

We felt like it was all spiralling out of control.

I remember sitting on watch one night and imagining our family at home going about their daily lives, eating meals, going to work, watching telly . . . all that ordinary stuff that we take for granted. It seemed like another universe. They were safe. I was in tears thinking how dear they all were to me. How much I wanted to see them again. How wonderful it would be to play Scrabble with my sister Pakeezah, to lay a puzzle with our son Simon, to read a bedtime story to our grandson Ford, to cook for Chris' dad, to hug my Mum, to share a meal with my brother Ole and my sister-in-law Rema.

I know . . . I had no right to feel sorry for myself. We had landed ourselves in this mess....No one else had made the choices that had gotten us here. I had always been a risk taker . . . an adventurer. In my ignorance, I had always looked down on the ordinary. But . . . I had never envisioned that my yearning for adventure would get me into this precarious position.

Somehow, if you are born in the Western world, you are arrogant enough to think that somehow you are special. Really bad stuff happens to the others. Even if worse comes to worst, you will be okay, the embassy will bail you out . . . the cavalry will show up. Okay, sometimes Westerners did get in trouble in the hotspots of the world. But they were usually military personnel, or journalists, people who put themselves in bad places due to their job. I wasn't one of them. I was just cruising the world minding my own business.

Yet . . . here we were. Not an embassy or cavalry in sight. We were truly alone. Just us and the pirates, and we knew we would get no mercy from them.

I wondered if I would ever feel safe again, and I promised myself that I would never again take my privileged life in safety for granted.

CHAPTER 23

And so we continued north, now back to the original plan of hugging the coast. We still had many miles to go until we were north of the last reported attack. The strategy was to keep heading toward Pakistan as fast as possible, to stay as invisible as possible, and to stay as close together as we could.

Staying close to *Libertad* turned out to be stressful in itself. We had quite a different sailing style, and they had a damaged winch, which made it difficult to sail efficiently into the wind. They had to tighten the foresail by hand, which only Juan had the strength to do. But he could not be on watch all the time. He needed sleep too, so sometimes they lagged behind.

On the other hand, there were times when they were ahead of us, and we had trouble catching up. Who knows?! In any case, we would sometimes get separated by a mile or so, during the day. I did not like it. I was so afraid of losing sight of them.

However, Chris was hell-bent on sailing *Skylark* as efficiently and as fast as possible. Understandable . . . we all wanted to get off that ocean. The reality was that, whatever progress either of us had made, by nightfall we needed to close the gap between the boats or risk losing each other altogether. On a couple of occasions this meant actually turning back on ourselves . . . losing some precious miles northward. This was really, really hard on Chris. It almost drove him to despair. He felt like we would never reach our goal. I took it more philosophically . . . trying to tell myself that the day's progress was only measured in the miles made by the slowest boat. We were in this together . . . we needed to regard *Libertad* as an extension of ourselves.

Chris and I are a couple that is usually in harmony. We have our moments, but they are truly rare. However, this trip really tested our relationship to the limit. We were just so scared and tired. A thing like having to retrace our steps and losing miles of progress could erupt into a screaming match. We did not recognise ourselves.

I have read stories about people who go through a horrible ordeal . . . like losing a child . . . and losing their marriage over it. I always thought that so strange. Surely going through something awful together should unite you . . . if anything. I now understand. When you are at your wit's end, you lash out at anyone around . . . like a caged animal. It does not necessarily bring out the best in you. We needed to support one another. It seemed we were doing just the opposite.

In many ways, blue water sailing is a mental ordeal. Ask any single-hander who has spent weeks at sea on their own. They often say that the conversation going on in their head is the hardest to bear . . . not the storms or other sailing challenges. When there is no one to talk to, the inner conversation can spiral out of control. Even when sailing as a couple, like us, or like Juan and Lucia, one spends a lot of time on one's own.

Certainly it seems that we all seemed to focus our fear in different directions.

For me, I latched on to the idea that we *must not* lose sight of *Libertad*. Rationally, I understood that they offered us no real protection, in fact possibly the opposite because of the weapons . . . but rationality has nothing to do with this. There were times when our VHF communication broke down . . . sometimes because we had gotten too far away from each other . . . sometimes because someone was using a handheld and the battery was gone. I think "freaked out" probably describes what happened to me at those times.

Chris, on the other hand, seemed to worry less about pirates than about the normal sailing concerns such as fuel consumption, gear failure, bad weather, and collision danger. Except that he magnified them. He was almost paranoid that something would go wrong with the boat. Every little noise that he had not heard before . . . seemed to him to spell disaster. On a calm day, he would anticipate a storm. At night every approaching ship threatened to run us over. He was on a constant adrenaline high.

We had turned off our AIS transmitter, and with no nav lights, we were invisible to the ships out there. So collision was a real danger. We should not have seen many ships, on the route we were on. Officially we were well out of the shipping lanes.

However, all the rules have changed in the Indian Ocean. The ships are also afraid to go through the middle, so like us, they were creating a new shipping lane which precisely followed the route we were taking . . . up the Indian coast. So . . . we saw a lot of ships. Most of them did not have any navigation lights on, but some kept on their AIS transmitter.

To start with, Chris followed our usual protocol, and would call up the ship on VHF to alert them of our presence. He also turned on some lights whenever he felt threatened by a ship. This became a point of conflict between us and *Libertad*. Juan felt that Chris was exposing us by these actions. Because . . . Juan's mental focus was on staying invisible.

Eventually, Juan won this point, and Chris had to stop communicating with ships.

But . . . before he did, there was an interesting conversation with one ship. After the usual talk with the captain of the vessel, alerting him of our presence, the captain handed the mike over to a chap with a cockney English accent.

He quizzed us about what we had seen in the area. "Have you seen any suspicious vessels? Have you heard any suspicious communication on the radio?"

Turns out he was the leader of the ship's mercenary crew. Many ships now hire groups of heavily armed mercenaries for the crossing of the Indian Ocean . . . .a boon industry for these ex-military chaps who want to continue doing what they know best.

So, I had separation anxiety; Chris had gear, weather, and collision concerns; Juan's bug-bear seemed to be stealth . . . and Lucia . . . she seemed to worry about Juan's well-being a lot.

In our conversations with Lucia, she had told us that for most of their sailing, it was Juan who did all of the night watches. He would only wake her up when he was absolutely exhausted and would then sleep next to her in the cockpit while she kept watch for a few hours. He also did most of the sail-handling. Most of their sailing had been shorter hops than this . . . so that system had worked quite well for them.

However, this was different. We were facing weeks at sea in challenging conditions. I don't want to portray Lucia as a helpless boat-wife who confined her skills to the galley . . . because she was not. In her land-job she was a high powered executive, and she certainly seemed to know her way around a boat. It was just the way they did things. She was perhaps more the navigator and planner, while he did most of the sailing.

They described their sail around the world as more of a "pointing the boat in the right direction and then relaxing." They did not care for speed or efficiency much.

In a sense we had been the same. We did not try to push *Skylark II* unnecessarily. But . . . this was a different deal. We had to be efficient . . . We had to sail those boats to the best of our ability . . . We had to push! We all wanted to get out of there as fast as possible.

So, it was a real challenge for them, especially for Lucia, to become more involved. In the beginning it did seem to be Juan who was always on watch at night, but we could hear his voice deteriorating into exhaustion over the radio. She was right to worry about him . . . and in the end she did take night watches.

She had to.

In any case, as well as facing the pirates, we all faced our inner demons. On those long nights on our own in the dark, we had too much time on our hands.

I can't presume to really know what was going on with the others . . . but for me, I think I have never felt quite as alone as on that trip. Even through my battle with cancer, there was comfort available, a sympathetic hug, someone stronger than me who could send some of their strength my way. I needed that help now . . . I needed a shoulder to cry on . . . I needed someone to tell me that it would be all right.

But . . . Chris was fighting his own fears. He was as much in need of comfort as I was. He had nothing to give. He was as depleted as I was.

This time, I was truly on my own. I had to dig deep to find the courage to get me through this.

Funny . . . isn't it? . . . I have so often been told by people that they think we were so brave to cross that ocean. Brave?! Hell no . . . We trembled in fear every step of the way!

CHAPTER 24

We continued north as fast as we could manage.

Our frayed nerves started to tell in our relationship on the radio with Lucia and Juan. Mostly we had enjoyed each other's company and joked around on the radio to lighten the mood. Now, things seem to have gotten more serious, grimmer.

We started to squabble about each other's sailing style.

"Why can't they keep up?"

" Why can't they wait for us?"

In reality, the boats were probably as well matched as any two very different yachts could hope to be. However, anyone who has tried to stay in close proximity with another yacht over miles of ocean can attest to how difficult a task that is. Add to that the stresses we were under, it is a feat in itself that we later parted on friendly terms.

As we approached the border between India and Pakistan, we again started to get concerned about diesel. Soon we would reach the point in the north Indian Ocean where we would have to cross over to the other side. This meant sailing very close to the pirate attack area. If necessary we wanted to be able to run from harm. We knew that if the pirates spotted us, we could not outrun them. However, if we saw them first, on radar for instance, we could try and head in the opposite direction. We did not want to be low on fuel if that were to happen. So the urge to refuel grew.

We decided to try our luck in India once more. Again we had no real information about the area, no cruising guides, and no proper charts.

What we did have was a CD, given to us by a cruiser in the Marshall Islands, which contained a copy of *Worldwide Sailing Directions*. Despite its name, this is a document that has nothing to do with sailing. It is a guide used by the merchant marine ships to give them basic information on available harbours. For instance, it roughly describes the harbour and the bunkering facilities there.

It wasn't much, but it was better than nothing. At least it gave us an idea of which harbours were around and the approximate size of the place. We wanted a place large enough to have a bank or an ATM machine, because we had no local currency to pay for fuel. On the other hand, we wanted a place small enough not to have too much officialdom on site. We did not want an official Port of Entry. The higher up in the chain of command the officials were, the more likely they would be to give us a hard time about not having visas.

In the end, we chose a place called Veraval and headed for the coast.

This time, we made a bad choice.

Like we had done before in Malpe, we anchored close to the harbour entrance. Soon, we were joined by a police boat.

They seemed friendly enough and told us "No problem." We could get fuel, but we had to follow them in to the harbour proper. They assigned an official to each of our boats. They said it was "to help us" . . . or perhaps to make sure we did not try to escape.

The inner harbour was fairly small. There were many scruffy local fishing boats rafted up to one another at the end of the harbour. There were a few filthy stone buildings, mostly ruins, with rusted corrugated iron roofs. A concrete bunker-like building on one end of the harbour, its walls green with mildew, flew an Indian flag from its roof . . . the police building. The water was little better than an open sewer . . . In fact it was a sewer. Human excrement floated about among the plastic water bottles and other unmentionable debris.

We later saw why. In the mornings we were greeted by naked brown backsides squatting at the edge of the harbour performing their morning ablutions into its filthy water.

Along one end of the harbour, there was a rough stone wall, black with grease and dirt, towering up some four metres from sea-level. This was where they wanted us to tie up.

This we did, and were soon the greatest show to have hit that town for years. The place was positively medieval, and they had certainly never seen a yacht before. At all times day and night while we were there, there were thirty to fifty people sitting and standing on the seawall above our boats, staring at us, commenting on us, trying to communicate with us, and unfortunately spitting betel nut juice, which soon stained our decks red.

This was all fine and well and even amusing to start with, but soon lost its appeal. Especially so, when the boats were visited by one official after another, probably thirty in all, who questioned us, searched the boats thoroughly, and left their black boot prints to supplement the betel nut stains on the decks and in the cockpit.

We were told we could not leave the boats, and we could not leave the harbour. In short, we were detained.

We tried to stay calm. We smiled and smiled . . . at everyone. We tried to engage the observing crowd in conversation.

Someone asked if we needed food. I said that I would love to buy some fresh fruit, maybe bread if there was any. Half an hour later, the guy came back . . . It turned out he was a local policeman . . . with a gift of fruit, veggies, and fish. He refused payment.

And so the first day passed, with us telling our story over, and over, and over again, to one group of officials after another.

In all this, Juan was a champion. He took the lead in talking to the authorities. He really had a great way about him. He was charm itself, listening carefully to what the officials were saying and answering with respect and courtesy.

There was a bit of a close call too. Juan and Lucia confessed to us later that they had initially not planned to mention the fact that they had weapons on board. However, as they sat in their cockpit talking to an official, they luckily saw that his colleagues, searching the boat below, were rooting around very close to the place where the weapons were hidden. They quickly slid the fact that they had weapons into the conversation, so that it could not be said later that they had tried to hide anything. They were asked to produce their licence for the guns, and did so.

We wondered later whether it was the weapons that caused us to be detained, but although I am sure it did not help the situation, it should not have been a factor. Many boats carry weapons, and you have every right to do so as long as they are licensed and you declare them upon entry.

We told ourselves that they were all just curious. That each official wanted an excuse to see the boats for himself.

Evening came, and still no word on whether we could buy fuel or not. It became obvious that nothing would happen that day. We decided to make the best of things and have drinks and dinner together. The two boats were rafted together, with *Skylark II* next to the stone wall and *Libertad* tied on to our starboard side. To increase the distance from the persistent crowd of observers on the quay, we decided to have a meal together on *Libertad*.

Although we had already shared quite a few adventures, we actually did not know each other well. We had only met Juan and Lucia briefly in Galle, Sri Lanka. We had a bit of a connection, because they were from South America, and I had lived in Brazil for awhile while growing up. I spoke Portuguese and Spanish and so did they. This turned out to be a bit of a boon for us, as we were able to talk on the radio in Portuguese, making it even harder for anyone listening in to understand what was being said.

Anyway, we had a pleasant evening in the cockpit. They were a really nice couple. They told us that they had recently married and this cruise around the world was almost a bit of a honeymoon. They were too young to be able to cruise indefinitely; in fact their cruising kitty had reached its end, and they were now making tracks to get back home to go back to work.

I think the evening was also an opportunity to clear the air a bit. As mentioned, things had started to get a bit tense out there. That evening we were able to laugh about each other's sailing style, about the things that had started to irritate us. We were two couples of different generations, but we were all sailors, and fate had thrown us into each other's company. We were determined to make the best of things.

However, by the afternoon of the second day of questioning, we had lost all sense of humour. That day, Juan and Chris were taken away to a police station to be questioned by the secret police, and Chris returned to *Skylark*, accompanied by officials and told me, wide-eyed with fright, that they wanted our laptops so forensic specialists could check on their contents. There had been mention of the need to contact our embassies, and we were seriously starting to wonder if we would end up in an Indian jail.

As luck would have it, Chris reported back that to his extreme relief, when the forensic specialists went into our laptop, the first thing they saw was an email from our leader, Phillip, urging us not to cross to Salalah but to continue north along the Indian coast until at least 23 degrees latitude, as the pirate danger was too great further south. This was exactly what Chris and Juan had been telling the police, so verified their story.

While we were waiting for developments later that afternoon, a huge wooden ship, perhaps seventy feet in length, beam of twenty feet, and topsides towering ten feet above us (akin to a Noah's Ark) decided to come in to the seawall where we were tied up. There was definitely not enough room for them and us on the same seawall, but this did not deter them in the slightest.

We were shouting for the bystanders to go get the police as we had been told in no uncertain terms that we could not move from there. No one reacted. In the end we would either be crushed or move, so we moved.

Juan, who had been patience itself with the officials up to that point, finally lost his cool and said to us, "Let's just get the hell out of here!"

That really scared me. I had visions of being chased by Indian Coast Guard gunboats. I pleaded with him to see reason and he did.

We anchored in the outer harbour and continued to wait for

word on our fate.

Evening came and we prepared for another night in captivity. Finally, after dark at 8 p.m., the original friendly police boat crew came out and announced that all was well; we had been given permission to refuel and leave.

Juan stayed with the boats, and the rest of us piled all our jerry jugs into the police boat and were taken ashore. There followed another interrogation, this time by a local journalist (we think), and then a bizarre refuelling operation. The jerry jugs went on the back of a motor-trike with a pickup-tray attached. Lucia and I were transported on a motorbike behind a police sergeant and Chris on a third bike behind another policeman.

The police sergeant spoke English well and told Lucia and I that the reason for our long detention in Veraval was that we were suspected of possibly being spies or terrorists for the Pakistanis. There had apparently been a British yacht involved in that kind of activity, not so long ago.

However, after a thorough investigation, they had decided that we were telling the truth.

We refuelled, got a couple of hours of sleep, and set off at crack of dawn the next morning, eager to see the last of Veraval and feeling lucky to be once again in the relative freedom of those pirate-infested waters.

CHAPTER 25

Soon after leaving Veraval, we had to leave the shores of the Indian subcontinent and head across the northern Indian Ocean toward Oman.

The pirate attacks had occurred farther and farther north, forcing us far beyond the original planned 20° latitude. We finally attempted the crossing at 23.5° north, along the coasts of Pakistan and Iran.

Just before leaving Indian territorial waters, we were over flown by an Indian Coast Guard Jet, who called us on VHF channel 16. He wanted to know if we were aware that we were heading into dangerous waters full of Somali pirates. Well . . . yeah!

His parting comment was "I admire your spirit of adventure."

The next four hundred miles were nerve-wracking. I don't think there was a single moment when we were not staring at the horizon expecting a skiff to appear and signal our doom.

We were now being even more careful to be invisible. Communications were really down to a bare minimum. I still felt that talking on the ham radio was pretty safe but Juan and Lucia thought that even these frequencies could be scanned by someone with the knowledge to do so, and they wanted to take no chances. Juan had gotten annoyed with us a couple of times when we had mentioned our destination by mistake. He also felt that we should stop our daily communication with *Bliss* and to not report our position to UKMTO any longer . . . just in case destination information slipped out. As *Bliss* and *Leah* were now safely in Muscat waiting for us, it would not affect them negatively not to communicate on a daily basis, so we informed them that we were stopping the radio schedule for the time being.

At about this time we got the news that Danish yacht *ING* had been captured with seven on board, three of whom were children. It was awful. We did not know them well, but we had met the skipper and had seen the children playing on the docks in Galle. Blond children...among them a beautiful blond girl, a teenager.

I remember the skipper, because he had attended a meeting in Galle. This was a meeting that Phillip had decided to call, to discuss the worsening situation in the Indian Ocean. He invited anyone who was attempting the crossing to attend, whether they were in our convoy or not. He felt that the situation had gone beyond the point of being coy about what information you held.

Whether you were a member of our convoy or not, we were all yachties in this together and he wanted to make sure all of us had as much information as possible. At the meeting, he showed the latest maps of where the attacks were happening and he explained why he thought it suicide to cross directly from the Maldives to Oman, as in previous years. He urged all who were there to take the longer route, skirting the sides of the ocean, north to Karachi and then across to Muscat.

Despite this warning, the crew of *ING* had decided to cross directly. They were taken hostage not far from the pirate stronghold of Suqutra Island, on their approach to the Omani Coast.

Now . . . I know that there has been a lot of criticism of the adults on *ING* in the media. Especially . . . people can't understand how any responsible parent could take children into that kind of danger.

I can certainly understand that criticism, but I guess knowing how we ourselves had ended up in peril despite making what we thought were logical decisions at the time, I have a bit more sympathy for them. They would never have taken their children into that kind of danger, if they had thought, even for a moment, that it could happen to them. I think there was just an innocence there. They must have believed the reports of piracy to be exaggerated. Perhaps, like us, they had been through many areas that were supposed to be dangerous and found them to be no problem. We all tend to use our past experiences as a guide to future decision-making. Their past experiences, like ours, told them it would be okay.

On the other hand I know that there were times when I wondered about Phillip and Lena bringing their beautiful eighteen month old daughter on this trip. I asked Lena about it once. She said, that they had thought about it long and hard. At one point they considered leaving her with family, for the duration of the trip. They felt quite strongly however, that if they were captured, eventually they would be released. At this stage no yachties had been killed by the pirates. The thought of spending months in captivity away from their daughter, to miss a year of her life, was worse. They decided that if they were to go through such an ordeal, they wanted to do it as a family. I know the worry caused Lena a lot of anguish though, throughout the trip. She was devastated when *ING* was captured, thinking about those children.

We all feared for the crew of *ING*. We had heard the stories. These pirates had no mercy, no sense of decency, no fair play.

Their only concern with us as being Westerners would be that they could perhaps extract a higher ransom. They were willing to cut off body parts to facilitate the process. They were animals. We had no rights. We felt incredibly alone and vulnerable.

I used to think about the pirates too. How was it that they had become like this? I still want to believe in the good in people. I want to believe that deep down we all just want to live our lives in peace. But . . . you do desperate things when you cannot feed your family. That is how it had all started . . . by some desperate starving Somali fishermen stumbling across an opportunity.

That . . . I could even understand . . . That . . . I could sympathize with.

But it had become big business. Now there were warlords, a type of super-rich mafia, involved. They supplied these poor fishermen with the weapons, with the grenades that they could never afford on their own. They sent them out there like soldiers in an army.

"Five thousand dollars to the first one to board a ship! Two thousand if you bring back hostages!"

This was a fortune to a poor Somali! He could feed his family on that for years! We had heard that they only supplied the skiffs with enough fuel to go out into the ocean. Not enough to get back. So, if you did not board a boat, you would starve and thirst to death. It is not the foot-soldiers; it is the organisers that are the truly evil people!

We were now closer to the pirate zone than we had ever been before. We were sneaking by just eighty miles from the place of an attack. We knew they were definitely out there, not far from us.

One night the VHF came to life, with a voice that did not belong to any of the four of us. It was the frightened voice of a radio officer aboard a merchant marine vessel, calling for help while his ship was being attacked.

"They have ladders! We have pushed them off, but they come again! Please! We need help!"

He then gave his co-ordinates and we quickly looked on the chart. The attack was happening about two hundred miles away. Normally a VHF transmission does not have that kind of range, but in certain conditions, you can pick up calls at a great distance. It was eerie to listen to the drama.

We had heard what would ordinarily happen in such an attack. The pirates would come alongside the vessel in several skiffs, small boats with very powerful outboard motors. They would put up ladders to help them climb aboard . . . a very tricky operation . . .

even on a calm day. Once they got aboard, they would gather up the crew and choose a crew-member . . . often the captain . . . and threaten to shoot him, then and there, if any of the crew offered any kind of resistance . . . such as disabling the engines or cutting the ship's power. Then they would order the captain to head for Somalia.

Once there, the ship would be anchored and the crew held on board while negotiations started with the owners and the insurance company. Sometimes the crew were taken off the vessel and held in a large "hostage concentration camp," but more often they were held in the hold and given just enough food and water to survive.

Typically a negotiation would take up to three months, but in the end, the pirates generally got their money. Unfortunately, both the insurance company and the owners would eventually relent as the ship and the cargo would usually be worth more than the millions asked in ransom.

The ships have devised some strategies to prevent this from happening. First of all, like us, they try to be invisible. If an attack happens, they often have mercenary crews on board to repel the boarders. They try to push off the ladders, pour hot liquids down, fire at the pirates, anything they can do. In the meantime, of course, they are trying to alert a Coalition warship of the attack, and hope that there is one close enough to come to the rescue. As a final means of defence, a lot of ships now have a "safe room" or "citadel" built into the structure of the ship. This is a reinforced bunker, where the crew can seek safety and wait out the pirates. The bunker would have survival supplies and radio communication, sufficient for a longer wait. The theory is that the pirates will eventually get nervous of an approaching Coalition vessel and give up.

These strategies do work, sometimes . . . and not all attacks on ships are successful.

"What about the defenders then?" I hear you ask.

"Where are all these Coalition forces? Why are they not coming to the rescue?"

It is complicated.

The Indian Ocean is the size of Europe . . . a very large area to patrol. But it's not just that. Let's say that by chance, we have a navy vessel right next to our yacht, when the pirates come for us. The pirates are private citizens; they are civilians, not military. It is not a crime for them to approach us. Until they actually pull out their weapons and try to board the boat, they are not committing an act of piracy. And . . . from the time we would see a skiff in the distance, to when they are alongside us, is only a matter of perhaps ten minutes. As soon as the pirates board the boat, the navy has to back off. Now, there is a "civilian hostage situation," and they cannot risk the lives of the hostages in an attack.

So, in effect, they can do nothing; the window of opportunity for them to take action is too small. And that is if they, by some miracle, would be alongside us at the time of attack. As it takes a little longer for the pirates to successfully get aboard a large ship, the window of opportunity is a little bigger, but even in that situation, there is not a lot they can do.

In effect, until someone changes the rules of engagement, and allows these good guys to really defend us, risks or no . . . they will only ever be efficient as a deterrent.

Even when the navy comes out in full force, as we later found out that they did for the doomed cruisers on yacht *Quest*, things can go horribly wrong. In their case, the presence of the navy might have contributed to their being shot. But . . . that is not my story to tell as I have heard about it only second hand.

Our good friend, author Fatty Goodlander, has written a terrific book called *Somali Pirates and Cruising Sailors*, in which he tells this story and many others and discusses the whole situation in depth. If the piracy issue interests you, I can recommend this book wholeheartedly.

Anyway, for us, the presence of the navy did not turn out to be much help. In fact the opposite. I have already told the story of that awful night when we ended up at the receiving end of a searchlight in the night, scaring us out of our wits.

On another occasion, this time in broad daylight, a Coalition forces aircraft flew over us. They were soon followed by a helicopter, which had obviously been sent out to investigate. The helicopter crew, to our horror, called us on high power VHF radio saying

"Two sailing yachts at position xxx latitude, xxx longitude (giving our precise position), please reply to Coalition forces helicopter overhead."

Wonderful! Here we were in full stealth mode trying to be invisible and they announced to anyone listening within hundreds of miles that there were two little yachts, just ripe for the taking, and giving our exact position! We really had mixed feelings about that one! Nice to know the "friendlys" are there, but a bit more discretion guys, please!

CHAPTER 26

We were now getting close to Muscat, where we knew there were at least two members of our former convoy waiting for us in the marina.

A marina! God . . . didn't that sound good!

We started to get excited about reaching Oman, the crossing of the Indian Ocean behind us. At the same time, we knew it was far from over. The next leg, along the Omani coast from Muscat south to Salalah, was every bit as dangerous, if not more, than what we had just accomplished.

The Omani coast used to be considered safe. Even a year before, this area was reported to be fine, as the Omani Coast Guard patrolled it regularly.

However, this had also changed. With the explosion of piracy and their success rate, the pirates had obviously become more confident. In any case, no fewer than five attacks had occurred, very close to the coast, in the month prior to our arrival. It was now a definite no-go area. Nevertheless we would have to traverse it.

We were therefore hoping to be able to sail together with the two boats waiting for us in Muscat, in a mini-convoy of four boats.

We had also had news of the Austrian brothers, Franz and Hans. They had towed *Serendipity* into Cochin. They had been forced out of Cochin as they had no visas and there was no emergency involving their boat, only *Serendipity*. So, they had left there a couple of weeks ago and made their way more or less along the route we had taken. Theirs was a racing yacht, and they knew how to sail it. We watched in astonishment at how fast they were catching up with us; in fact, before we reached Muscat, they passed us. We had hoped that they also would join our mini-convoy from Muscat to Salalah, but they decided to not stop.

Franz told us that he felt that if they stopped in Muscat, he might find it difficult to find the courage to set off once more. He preferred to be scared all in one go and just do the extra days required to get to Salalah, before allowing himself to relax. In any case, they continued down the coast and we watched anxiously as they traversed this dangerous bit all by themselves. They made it though, and promised us that they would be waiting for us in Salalah, with a "big steak and a cold beer."

During the crossing, our thoughts had more and more turned to the immediate future. Where are the other boats? Will there be a convoy from Salalah to Aden as planned?

When we had parted from the other four boats that left the Maldives, plans were still to get together somewhere, at that time Karachi, to continue the journey in company. When Karachi fell through, the next meeting place was going to be Muscat. We also knew that a few other yachts had left the Maldives before we even got there, and that some of them had said they would wait in Salalah. And what about the leader? Where is Phillip? Is there in fact still a convoy of sorts, or are we on our own?

Juan and Lucia had similar thoughts, and it became clear in our conversations with them that they had become more and more disillusioned with the convoy. They felt abandoned and left to their own resources. So much so, that they were leaning toward doing their own thing anyway, even if there was a chance to join up with others.

Instead, they were investigating the possibility of asking a friend of theirs to join them, as a third member of their crew, for this last dangerous bit. I think part of their reasoning had to do with their need for haste. They were in a hurry and had already been delayed. They did not want to contemplate sitting around in some port waiting for the lead boat to arrive. Fair enough! However, they seemed to be banking on Chris and I following their lead and continuing alongside them.

We were torn. On the one hand, we had become a team. We had gone through a lot together with Juan and Lucia. It felt wrong to go our separate ways now. On the other hand, we were still desperate for the safety of a larger group of boats.

But, would there be a larger group? That was the question.

We decided to send out an email via ham radio to all the boats we thought might still be around, to try and gauge their intentions. The reply was heartening. Phillip replied that he was actually on his way across the Indian Ocean, probably no more than a week behind us. *Bliss* and *Leah* promised to wait for us in Muscat. Franz and Hans said they would definitely hang on in Salalah and told us that there were at least three other boats waiting for us.

This was good enough for us. We made our decision and told Juan and Lucia we would be heading for Muscat to rendezvous with the others. Shortly thereafter, they received the news that their friend would be joining them in Muscat, so they too would be aiming for there.

The last twenty-four hours approaching Muscat were so frustrating! We felt we could almost reach out and touch the safety of that marina. Mentally we were there already, sitting by the pool, sipping a cold drink. In safety! No pirates to worry about . . . at least for a few days!

It still seemed like an alternate universe and we reached and reached out for it mentally.

In the real world however, we were still plagued by the strong headwinds that had followed us all the way from the Maldives. We had thought that we would at least have winds on the beam after turning the corner to cross over . . . but no! The wind shifted and yet again we were battling into it.

It started to look like there would have to be another night at sea, another night among the pirates. We just couldn't go fast enough to reach Muscat by dusk.

By mid-afternoon, Juan had had enough. He turned on his engine and pushed the throttle forward to maximum revs.

Chris, ever cautious about the well-being of the engine and propeller, did not want to follow his lead, but in the end relented. The whole boat vibrated with the strain of the high revs, but we made it into Muscat harbour, just as the sun was setting.

It was a sight for sore eyes! Rugged mountains devoid of trees formed a stark but beautiful backdrop to the soaring towers of the blue-tiled minarets and the startlingly white buildings surrounding them. A graceful Arab dhow was anchored in the middle of the harbour. On shore, men in their flowing white robes strolled along the promenade, black-clad and veiled women at their side. True, there were some chrome and glass modern buildings and, on the right, a modern commercial port, but the general first impression of Muscat was like something out of a storybook. This was *Thousand and One Nights* stuff! I felt a glimmer of interest stir in my battle-weary soul.

We were not here to be tourists . . . but . . . wow . . . what a place!

After clearing in, we spent the first night at anchor in Muscat Harbour. The marina, where the others were waiting, was a few miles down the coast and we needed daylight to get there. But we did not mind. The main thing was that we were safe.

I keep saying that . . . I know . . . but that is my overriding memory of this time. Nothing mattered; absolutely nothing was as important . . . as being able to just turn off the constant worry in my head. Even if it was just for a few days, I needed rest from the worry. I needed to feel normal . . . for just a little while. I needed for that lump in my stomach that had been there since leaving the Maldives, all those weeks ago, to just dissipate.

We sat in the cockpit and watched the beauty of the many lights on shore and fell into our bunks, knowing that we would have the luxury of an uninterrupted sleep.

The following morning, we headed around the coast and into the marina.

Yet again, we were thrown into a different, yet familiar, environment. The marina was modern, with all the facilities you would expect from such a place. We could have been anywhere in the world. And there . . . were *Leah* and *Bliss* . . . welcoming us in!

CHAPTER 27

Here a really bizarre part of the story commences. Within a day of our arrival at the marina in Muscat, Juan and Lucia's new crewmember arrived. Their friend Jeremy had grown up in a military family. Right from the start it was obvious that he was a "larger than life" kind of person with a very strong personality. He soon interjected that strong personality into our plans of how to proceed for the next leg. That's putting it mildly. In truth, he took over. And somehow, we let him.

Already at our first informal planning meeting, Jeremy made it clear that we needed to forget any notions of not offering resistance in case of attack.

"The people on *Quest* have been killed! The situation has changed! We have to fight back!"

" It's the only way! We need weapons!"

Soon he had assigned the duty of ramming the pirates to the two aluminium boats, *Skylark* and *Leah*. In the meantime, he was going to show us how to manufacture Molotov cocktails and we'd have a practice session of throwing them. Better still, he would find Styrofoam pellets and add them to the Molotov cocktails "so that the fire sticks to the skin of the victim," in essence a napalm bomb.

Picture this: a cardiologist, a general practitioner, and an internist (all of whom had taken a vow to heal, not harm), a retired engineer and accountant, a lawyer, a boat builder, and a photographer, all sitting poolside in a marina in Muscat, sipping drinks and learning the how-to's of making and throwing Molotov cocktails.

It was utterly bizarre and it fills me with shame that Chris and I allowed ourselves to even consider such tactics. In our defence, I think the two of us were so shell-shocked and weary after the many weeks of stress that we were looking favourably at anyone who had the energy to suggest as to how we could get out of this mess.

We were weak, he was strong. He took over. We let him.

I have to add here that this was my impression of what happened. Penny and Paul on *Bliss* later told me that they never considered Jeremy a leader and just put up with his bluster to be polite, as he was a guest on one of the boats. They also had the advantage of being rested as they had been in Muscat for a week or so already, so were perhaps not as susceptible to Jeremy and his powers of persuasion as we were.

Nonetheless, every convoy has to have a leader, and Penny and Paul's doubts about Jeremy aside, he did take on that role. True to his word, Jeremy went "shopping" and came back with cases of vinegar in glass bottles and a huge sack of Styrofoam pellets. He emptied out the vinegar and refilled the bottles with petrol. He showed us how a spoonful or two of Styrofoam in each bottle changed the colour of the fuel as they melted. Now, the fuel had taken on the nature of napalm and would stick to the skin of the intended victim so that they could not extinguish the flames once they had been set alight.

I watched in morbid fascination as he then tied a rag around the neck of each bottle and explained that we would need to keep a container of fuel handy in the cockpit and dip the rag in fuel, set it alight, and throw the whole thing at the pirates.

I went back to *Skylark* feeling sick. Literally feeling ill. It was hard enough to envision us turning our bows into an approaching vessel and trying to ram it. It was just about beyond me to imagine myself putting a match to a Molotov cocktail and lobbing it at the pirates. I tossed and turned sleeplessly that night, trying to reconcile myself to the necessity of this. Never mind the horrible moral implications of trying to burn or kill someone, there was also the practical side. I had never been a good thrower and I could just imagine myself trying to light a fuel-soaked rag in the cockpit under stress. It would end up all over me, the cockpit, and the boat. Not just the pirates would be set alight. I could foresee a total disaster. Chris felt the same. We are peaceful people. We have never wanted to even carry a gun with us, because we firmly believe that if you carry a gun, you must be prepared to use it . . . and we are not. I did not hate the pirates. I feared them. They were people too . . . with families. I did not want to kill them. I just wanted them to leave us alone.

The next day, Jeremy stopped by our boat to visit. Over a cup of coffee he told us how he knew how to build a bazooka from scratch . . . had done it as a boy . . . with his brother. We just kind of nodded politely . . . not encouraging but also not discouraging him in his ravings.

I say ravings . . . because now . . . in hindsight . . . I think the guy was a bit nuts. My feeling was that he really wanted a battle. Bring it on! He did not actually say that, but it was the distinct impression I got when listening to him. To him this whole thing seemed like a bit of a lark and he was gung-ho for a fight.

I have always, I suppose superstitiously, believed that you must be careful what you think, because you can cause it to happen. I know . . . the more rational of you is now saying "Poppycock!" However, Chris and I had found that the longer we were in that awful stressful situation, the more superstitious we got. You didn't care to be rational anymore. If we had owned a rabbit's foot, we would have probably worn it around our necks . . . on the "you-never-know" principle. In any case, it worried me that he was spoiling for a fight . . . bad vibes!

In the end, Chris and I decided to tell Jeremy that we were not comfortable with the whole Molotov cocktail thing. We would be prepared to ram, but did not feel we wanted to be part of the bombardment. He was pretty good about it, saying we could carry a couple of cocktails, but did not need to carry an armoury of them. Penny and Paul came to the same conclusion, so in the case of an attack, it would have to be *Leah* and *Libertad* who were the "gun ships.".

At the final meeting in Muscat, we decided on the formation and the convoy rules. We would travel in a sort of diamond formation, with *Libertad* as lead boat. *Bliss* and *Skylark* would stay side by side behind them, and *Leah* would make up the rear. Jeremy insisted on a no VHF, no ham radio/SSB rule. Instead we would communicate by walkie-talkies. Gerhardt had found that he had four of these on *Leah*, so we tuned them all to the same frequency and took aboard one each. They had a range of only about fifty metres, so we would really have to stay very close to be able to communicate. We were not allowed to use our VHF radios at any time.

Jeremy also did not want anyone using their deck-level navigation lights at night. Originally, we had all put black tape over most of these deck-level navigation lights, so only a sliver would show, but Jeremy thought that was still too visible. We would use a small white light encased in a sock. Obviously we were not allowed to put on our masthead lights for any reason.

To reduce our visibility in the daytime, we were not going to sail at all during daylight hours. Jeremy thought that a sail could be seen from too far away. So, we would only use our motors in the daytime. Possibly we would be able to use our sails at night, to enhance our speed. There was a bit of grumbling about this, as most of us sail faster than we motor, but in the end, we all agreed to it.

Finally, we decided on a route. We were to literally hug the coast, staying within the twelve metre depth contour at all times. This meant a longer route, as we could not cross some of the deeper bays. Instead we would go into each bay. The idea was that the pirates would probably be further out, so it was safer to stay close to shore. Of the five reported attacks in that area in the preceding two months, one had been within eight miles of the shore, so we felt we had to stay even closer than that, if possible.

We left the meeting feeling the anxiety levels increase again. If anything, it felt even harder to face going out there again, after a week of safety. The leg to Salalah from Muscat was a good six hundred miles, so it would take us anywhere from five days to a week. It seemed a long way! I suppose being closer to shore should have been comforting, but instead I felt that in the case of an attack from the sea, we would be hemmed in by the land . . . nowhere to run to. However, there certainly was a comfort in being four boats instead of two.

Anyhow, like it or not . . . we had to do it . . . so with that sinking feeling in the pit of my stomach again, we waved goodbye to Muscat and set off.

CHAPTER 28

Already the first night out of Muscat, there was trouble.

The strategy of hugging the coast put us into the hundreds of fishing nets dotted about the coast. They were unlit and marked only by a piece of Styrofoam . . . there was no way to see them.

Soon, we were caught. The rest of the convoy had to stop and loll about while poor Chris had to dive into the black waters under the boat and clear the nets from the rudder. He was trying to be brave about it, but I could see that he was horrified at the thought of getting into that water in the middle of the night, with the waves plunging the stern platform up and down, and the boat still making a bit of way in the current. Apart from worrying about any sharks or other sea critters about, I was terrified that he would get caught in the net and never surface. It was horrible. All I could do was try and shine a torch into the water. We thought about attaching a line around his waist, but he felt it would probably be in the way. However, he succeeded and we rejoined the others, with great difficulty as they were now too far away to see their lights and had been swallowed up by the night.

Now we had something else to be paranoid over, the fear of catching another net. We suggested we head a little further offshore, at least during night hours, but this was vetoed by Jeremy. He preferred the fishing nets to the increase in risk of heading out. We had to follow.

It was a strange thing to us, but whenever there was a communication from *Libertad*, it was always Jeremy on the radio. We were used to talking to Juan and Lucia, but it almost seemed as if they had disappeared . . . never a word from them. After all, Juan was still the skipper of *Libertad* and Jeremy was supposed to be crew. We could only assume that they had agreed to let him be skipper on this part of the trip.

The nightmare with the fishing nets continued. Apart from *Libertad*, which is a full-keel boat, which tends to allow the nets to slip off, all of the rest of us had to deal with being caught in nets at regular intervals. This really slowed us down, as each time someone was caught, we all had to stop and wait and then regroup, often losing up to an hour with each incident. It was madness. We longed to head further offshore, but Jeremy wasn't having it.

The lack of navigation lights was also turning out to be an issue. The small lights we did use were just about useless, unless you were almost on top of the neighbouring boat. It is very hard to judge distances at night, and with four of us out there jostling for position, there was a real danger of collision. Chris and I resorted to using our radar, although Jeremy had stated that he was not happy with anyone using the radar, as he felt that the pirates might have radar detectors. Nonetheless, at least the radar gave us a picture of where the other boats were and how close, so it was some comfort.

Keeping station using the radar was almost like playing some kind of computer game, though quite exhausting. We were endlessly measuring our distance to the others to see if we needed to slow down or speed up or change course to stay in our assigned position. Watches were tense and demanding . . . certainly no time for relaxation over a cup of coffee. If you let down your guard for even a couple of minutes, you might find yourself too close or too far away from the others.

On day two, about mid-morning, the VHF babble in Arabic was interrupted by a familiar voice.

"*Skylark II*, *Skylark II*. This is *Serendipity*. Do you copy?"

We could hardly believe it! *Serendipity*! Our lead boat! We thought she was still sailing up the coast of India, after her repair stop in Cochin!

I remember feeling confused. I wanted to answer, wanted to badly, but this was against Jeremy's rule of No VHF!

I dithered while *Serendipity* kept calling us. In the end *Bliss* broke the rules and answered.

Indeed it was *Serendipity* and she had caught up with us after a marathon sail across the Indian Ocean. They were only a few miles away and we were heading toward them. Within an hour we rendezvoused. Cheers all around.

But wait . . . she was carrying sails, and it was daylight. This was against our rules. I was volunteered to explain our rules to them. I could tell that Phillip was unimpressed, especially when I told him about the Molotov cocktails, but he replied that, as we had already formed our own mini-convoy and set our strategies, they would follow on behind and abide by our decisions.

We had another couple of walkie-talkies on *Skylark*. They were on another frequency, but we handed one to *Serendipity*, which enabled contact between *Skylark* and *Serendipity*, but they were unable to communicate with the rest of the boats. And so we proceeded.

When *Serendipity* joined us, we noticed that they had two new crew members on board. It turned out that these were two Dutch cameramen who had asked Phillip for permission to join *Serendipity* for the sail across the Indian Ocean and Red Sea. They were producing a documentary on piracy for a Dutch current events program. Phillip had told us in advance in Thailand that they might join *Serendipity*, and at the time we thought it a good idea, as we thought it might encourage the naval forces to put their best foot forward and accompany our convoy.

This ended up not being the case . . . We had no help from any Coalition forces . . . but the camera crew provided another advantage . . . They provided us with professional footage of our trip in the form of a DVD, something we now treasure. But . . . I am getting ahead of myself again!

At this point we were all pretty much taking orders from Jeremy. As is sometimes the case with people of very strong character, his leadership sometimes bordered on the abusive. He started talking to us as though we were errant children who refused to toe the line.

This was brought to a head the second night. It was a very dark night and almost impossible to make out the boats surrounding you. Especially Chris, who has very poor night vision, was struggling to stay with the fleet. We thought we had agreed to a certain route, but *Libertad* seemed to be drifting away from it, getting closer to the coast.

When we asked Jeremy to give us his course and speed so we could stay together, he replied aggressively "If you would just get your heads away from the computer screens and look out into the night, you would maybe be able to spot me."

He refused to give us a course and speed and said he was "sailing to the wind" and he expected us to just follow. His tone indicated that we were bothering him with our requests for course and speed.

This was the final straw. Finally we had had enough.

Paul, on *Bliss*, put on his low-level, tape-covered navigation lights, so that Chris and I could see to follow him.

Jeremy immediately screamed over the walkie-talkie "Turn off that f...ing light immediately! You have just given away our position to any pirate within miles!"

Paul calmly replied something to the effect that we were actually experienced sailors out here, and he could not recall anyone formally agreeing to make Jeremy the elected leader. In his opinion we were running an unacceptable risk of collision sailing without decent lights, in close proximity of other boats. His lights were staying on!

Jeremy replied, "In that case you are on your own!"

"No problem," Paul replied. "*Skylark*, follow us. This is our course and speed."

We continued through the night and it was a dream following *Bliss*. Penny and Paul gave calm and precise directions in a civilized manner. We were very relieved. Despite Jeremy's bluster that we could make our own way if we did not follow his rules, we could see that *Libertad* continued following the convoy, albeit at a distance and without another word on the radio.

This was "Leadership Coup Number One." Another was to follow.

Phillip on *Serendipity*, although unable to hear the conversations between the boats, was nonetheless observing the progress of the convoy, the near collisions, the boats captured in fishing nets in the night, etc.

On the morning after the ousting of Jeremy's leadership, Phillip broke the VHF rules and called all boats for a VHF conference. Basically, he relayed what he had observed, why he thought some of our rules did not work, and why he thought that we were endangering ourselves by these rules. He said that he would not continue on with the convoy in its present format, but would rather carry on alone. He would use low-level navigation lights at night, use sails whenever possible to hasten the trip (even in daylight), would speak on low power VHF only as much as was absolutely necessary, and would not agree to active resistance in case of an attack. Anyone wishing to follow with him was welcome. He wished the rest a safe passage and "see you in Salalah."

Skylark, *Bliss*, and *Leah* immediately agreed to follow his lead.

A few minutes later, a familiar voice that we had not heard for a while, Lucia on *Libertad*, got on the radio and said that they wanted to tag along too. They reported that they had thrown the Molotov cocktails overboard and they would agree to the passive approach in case of attack.

Thus ended "Leadership Coup Number Two."

We don't know what went on aboard *Libertad* that day, but obviously Juan and Lucia were now back in charge, as we did not hear Jeremy on the radio at all for the remainder of that trip.

The next couple of days were relatively uneventful, although we did listen in to another pirate attack on a large ship on the VHF. We could hear the conversation between the harried radio operator and a Coalition warship, who unfortunately was two hundred miles away and unable to help.

We did have daily scares, as the area was full of fishing skiffs.

Each time Phillip would alert us to the danger and ask us to close up ranks. Each time, I resorted to my list of "Procedures in Case of Pirate Attack" and went below and put on my long trousers. The others saw me appearing with long trousers on and soon asked why. I explained and everyone had a good laugh. It became a standing joke . . . some light relief. As soon as an alert went out I could see the binoculars trained on *Skylark* to see if I was wearing my trousers!

Luckily, each time we were able to stand down after awhile, when we could determine that the skiffs contained two to three persons and they were followed by large flocks of sea birds, a sure sign of a fishing vessel.

On the last day, before our arrival at Salalah, our luck almost ran out.

It was about mid-day, when we got the call from *Serendipity*, "Skiffs at twelve o'clock and three o'clock. Close up, guys."

This was now almost a routine call. However, this time it was different. Soon we were surrounded by four skiffs, each with nine to ten men in them. The skiffs were newer looking, freshly painted. There were no sea birds. And they acted differently. The skiffs circled the convoy at a distance. Two of the skiffs stopped and had a mid-ocean conference. Then they went and spoke to one of the other skiffs. This was not the behaviour of fishermen. There was a purpose to their actions.

We could do nothing except huddle together as close as possible in our five boat convoy. We were probably no further than five metres apart and picking up speed as fast as the slowest boat would allow. Anxiety was tangible. There was no doubt in any of our minds that this was the real thing. These were Somali pirates and they were debating how to go about attacking our little fleet.

On the premise that the pirates might have VHF radios as well, Phillip made a great show of picking up his hand-held VHF and as loudly as possible issuing a Mayday call.

"Mayday! Mayday! We are five yachts at such and such latitude and longitude and we are surrounded by 4 pirate skiffs. They are preparing to attack us. We need urgent assistance!!"

None of us thought the Mayday call would actually bring us any kind of help. As far as we knew all Coalition vessels were many hundreds of miles away. However, we hoped that the pirates did not know that.

They continued to circle and debate for about an hour and a half. The knot in my stomach just grew and grew. When I was about ready to scream, the skiffs just disappeared out to sea over the horizon, presumably back to their mother ship. Relieved?! That's putting it mildly!

This situation . . . this exact situation . . . is why anyone silly enough to attempt to cross these pirate-infested waters *must* travel in convoy. If we had been on our own, we would, without the slightest doubt, have been hostages in Somalia now. A lone boat does not stand a chance. What kept these pirates from attacking was that we were five. They do not know if any of those boats carry weapons and can shoot them in the back while they try to attack one of us. Also, they know that there will be an immediate call for help from the boats that are not under attack. They could not assault all five of us at once. It was numbers that saved us.

The next day we arrived in Salalah in Oman on the Yemeni border. We all heaved a sigh of relief.

Ironically, in previous years, this had been the starting point of the dangerous bit. This was where boats gathered to form convoys after crossing the Indian Ocean alone.

But, by 2011 all this had changed. The stretch Salalah (Oman) to Aden (Yemen) is now quite well patrolled and although attacks happen there still, the most dangerous part of the journey is now the crossing of the Indian Ocean.

So we felt that the worst was behind us. Nonetheless, local wisdom was still that it was far too dangerous to do the Yemeni coast except in convoy. In fact the large ships also formed convoys here, with up to twenty huge ships travelling together for safety, usually with a prearranged naval vessel to accompany them.

It was premature to start feeling safe.

CHAPTER 29

In Salalah, the convoy grew to nine boats, as some of the original thirty boats of our convoy had made their own way there and had waited for us. It was now mid-March and quite late to be heading into the Red Sea. In previous years, convoys had started from Salalah in either early or late February, so we were definitely behind schedule. This could mean windier conditions in the Red Sea . . . but that seemed a distant problem at that time. All we wanted was to put the pirates behind us.

Also in Salalah were the remnants of the Blue Water Rally boats, those that had made it across in safety. *Quest* had been part of this rally, and as could be expected, the rally participants we met were in shock and mourning for their friends on *Quest*. They had had a memorial service for the crew of *Quest* some days before, and at this service an official from UKMTO had spoken to them of the dangers of the next leg to Aden. They had decided *en masse* to go no further. They were all waiting for their boats to be loaded onto a ship and freighted to the Med.

They also saw it as their mission to try and prevent further tragedies and exerted a lot of pressure on us to join them in being transported. We understood their reasoning, but it made it an even more nervous time for us who were forced to give the Red Sea a go.

For us, it again came down to money. We simply did not have the US$30,000 required to ship our boat.

Salalah was an odd place to be. We were moored, bow anchor down and stern lines tied to the rocks, in an inner bay of a very large commercial harbour. We were a long way from anywhere, the town of Salalah being about a half hour's car journey away. Everywhere was dry, dry, dry, and barren. We were basically in the desert.

On the first night there, a sandstorm covered the decks and rigging in fine red sand, most of which would stay with us long after our arrival in Turkey. From now on, even if you dusted daily, all surfaces inside and outside the boat would have a fine covering of sand. It got into every nook and cranny and soon our ropes and lines got stiff with sand, dirt, and salt-spray. When I climbed my ratlines to get a better view, my hands, having touched the rigging wires, would come away filthy. We knew that we would not see rain for many months to come, so would have to live with this new challenge for the foreseeable future.

Nonetheless, Salalah had some decent supermarkets, and we were able to buy extra diesel there.

The latter was, in itself, a bit of an adventure. Diesel is very cheap in Oman . . . if you are a local. Our agent Mohammed, with his flowing white robes and ingratiating smile, wanted us to buy diesel from him . . . but at three times the price. We thought this a bit unfair. Perhaps double might be okay . . . but three times the price?! So we connived to smuggle some diesel in from the town.

The problem was that Mohammed was in cahoots with the guards who were authorized to search cars entering the harbour area. He told us we would be in *big trouble* if we were caught bringing diesel in.

Even so, most of us risked it. We rented a car and drove through the gates back and forth a few times so that the guards started to recognize us and got bored with searching us each time. Then we made our move . . . Diesel jugs in the trunk . . . covered by groceries. It set the heart racing a bit . . . but we were, after all, by now veterans of racing hearts . . . and we made it!

About a week later, we set off toward Aden in a convoy of nine boats. We all had assigned positions and code names. The code names were to confuse any pirates listening in. By using codes they could not determine if this foreigner speaking on the VHF was a small boat or a ship or even a military vessel. *Skylark II* was *Bravo 3*. There were also codes for our destinations, so if you were asked to give your position you did not give a latitude and longitude. Instead you had to say "We are 350 miles due west of Charlie."

As I have mentioned before, sailing in convoy is an exhausting exercise at the best of times, especially at night. You cannot relax, even for a moment, as you are very close to other boats. At least this time we were travelling with reduced deck-level navigation lights, but it was still very hard to judge distances at night. You are constantly forced to make adjustments to course and speed to try and maintain your position in the convoy. It takes hours to find the right course/speed combination and as soon as you do, the boats you are trying to stay in position with may make an alteration to their course or speed and you are back to square one.

So far I am talking about adjusting course and speed while under motor. Now imagine that the wind picks up and everyone starts sailing or motor-sailing.

A boat under sail has neither a constant speed, nor a constant course. Adjusting the speed is no longer a simple matter of pulling back on the throttle. Instead you roll sails in and out, try to spill wind to slow down, etc. It is extremely demanding.

If the wind picks up and is on the nose, the fun really begins. Now you have nine boats in close proximity all trying to tack, cross each other, etc., and all in the dark. It is havoc!

This happened a couple of times, and we were basically forced to break up the convoy and do our own thing until morning. The next day it took hours for all the boats to reconvene into formation.

Even so, for me it was wonderful to be surrounded by this many boats. I would take the stresses of convoy-sailing any day over being alone with just one other boat in the Indian Ocean! Everything is relative . . . isn't it?!

Apart from the stresses of sailing in convoy, the most worrying thing about this passage was the reports of political unrest that had been filtering through. We were travelling along the Yemeni coast, aware that this was a country on the verge of civil war.

Just a fortnight ago people had been killed during violent protests in the capital Sana'a and in the port town of Al Mukalla, where we were planning to stop as it was halfway between Salalah and Aden. Would we be welcome there? Some of us felt that we should give Al Mukalla a miss and head straight for Aden, but Phillip wanted to give it a go, as he knew that even after just a couple of days of convoy sailing we would all be very tired, especially the older couples. He reasoned that even one night's good rest could make the difference in being able to be alert for the remainder of the journey.

As we approached Al Mukalla harbour and set about anchoring in front of the town, we could hear chanting in the distance. First I thought it was some kind of prayer, but soon realised that we were witnessing a political demonstration, flags, slogans, and all. Nonetheless, we anchored and were soon approached by a gunboat. The commander told us that we could not anchor in front of the town, as the demonstrators were armed and might take pot-shots at the "foreign boats." Instead he urged us to go into the commercial port which was surrounded by fences and guarded twenty-four hours a day. We complied and rafted up as best we could in the tiny harbour.

Phillip and Lena spent hours pleading with the officials to at least let us go into the town for an evening meal. Lena had a secret weapon in her negotiations: her beautiful blond baby daughter. Even the sternest of the officials could not resist smiling at the antics of this lovely blue-eyed child.

After several false starts, they agreed, but only if we went all together in a bus escorted by a jeep filled with soldiers brandishing machine guns and bazookas. We ladies had to wear demure clothes and cover our heads with scarves. They took us to the Yemeni version of Kentucky Fried Chicken, not exactly what we would have chosen, but never mind. They also would not let us leave the restaurant. The Dutch camera crew tried to get away to take some footage of this medieval town, but were firmly brought to heel by the guards. At least there were no incidents and we did get a decent night's sleep.

CHAPTER 30

The next stop was Aden, which has a huge commercial port.

Once more we were uncertain whether we would be allowed to stop there. Just weeks before, a fellow yachtie had been forced to leave in a hurry when shooting erupted in the town. The officials had told him he had better up-anchor and leave, and he did not hesitate to follow their advice. However, Phillip thought it was worth a try, just to get some rest. We anchored in front of the town and went to clear in at the Customs/Immigration office in the harbour.

Here we had our first encounter with officials high on *khat*. Pretty much all men in Yemen chew this mild narcotic, which comes in the form of leaves. Many have chewed it for so long that the habit has caused their cheeks to balloon out into grotesque proportions. In any case all the officials were chewing away, and it was not uncommon to find them asleep at their post.

It was a bit eerie dealing with officials who are quite obviously high on drugs. Anyway, no one gave us any trouble except to ask for bribes, and when we did not comply with this, they felt fully justified in keeping our favourite pen despite our protests.

In previous years, Aden had been the place to celebrate a safe passage through the pirates.

Not so for us. We learned that quite a few attacks had been reported in the last couple of months on the next stretch of coast, between Aden and Bab al Mandeb. So we were not home free yet.

Even so, the stop in Aden was quite pleasant. Once more, we women had to dress conservatively and wear headscarves. My overriding memory of Aden was that the place was filthy with rubbish everywhere. Chris and I pride ourselves in always being willing to try the local restaurants . . . and did so in Aden as well. However, despite choosing the cleanest-looking restaurant on the waterfront, it was by far the dirtiest place in which I have ever eaten. Still, we did not get sick.

We were also able to do a little sightseeing. We visited a mosque, ancient water cisterns, and the market. Everywhere there was evidence of the ongoing political unrest. There were soldiers with machine guns all over the place as well as armoured vehicles and even tanks at some of the intersections. While in the market we could hear another demonstration approaching. Our guide nervously ushered us into the old market building and told us not to speak or look anyone in the eye. We complied without question.

Word was that Al Qaeda had taken the power in Aden. We were not going to mess with them!

After a week's rest, we set off again, for the last pirate-infested leg to Bab al Mandeb and into the Red Sea. This part of the journey brings you within twenty miles of the Somali coast, a fact that hangs over you like a dark cloud. It was kind of like travelling down a funnel, with the two coastlines of Yemen and Somalia converging on us. We knew that there had been several attacks right at the entrance to Bab al Mandeb.

For me it was once again tough mentally because we were now so very close to the relative safety of the Red Sea. My mind reached out to that safety and it was hard to stay in the moment. We had been in danger from those pirates for so long and it was almost over. I wanted to ignore today and just focus on tomorrow. I wished I could just go to sleep and wake up in the Red Sea.

However, there were still a few miles to go, and in the end we got through without incident. As it happened, as we got closer to the turning point, we were too busy with strong winds to worry too much.

Bab al Mandeb, the entrance to the Red Sea, is famous for its strong winds and currents. The name means "Gate of Tears," for the many voyages that have ended in disaster here throughout the centuries.

We did get the strong winds all right, but fortunately from behind. We shot through the entrance with thirty to forty knots of wind dead astern. Once through, it got even more "fun" as we made our first acquaintance with the short, steep waves for which the Red Sea is famous. In howling wind, we crossed the busy shipping lane toward the western shore.

Just as we were starting to feel that a celebration was coming on, there was a final challenge.

Our lead boat, *Serendipity*, once again had a problem with her propulsion, and was dead in the water drifting toward rocks. The Austrian brothers on *Geliebte*, coming to her rescue with a towline, suddenly developed an engine issue as well; their engine quit. Gerhardt on *Leah* then announced that he would come to the rescue but promptly hit a fishing net and was taken out of action. The rest of us were either too small or too far away to be much help and could only watch as that beautiful boat seemed to be sure to hit the rocks.

In the last minute, Franz on *Geliebte* managed to get their engine going and got *Serendipity* under tow. Even so, it was a close thing, whether the much smaller *Geliebte* would be able to make headway against thirty to forty knots of headwind towing the sixty foot, twenty-five ton *Serendipity*. Somehow they managed it. The wind was so strong that even without a boat to tow, *Skylark* barely made headway with motor running at max revs and a small headsail. Never a dull moment!

An hour later we were all extremely relieved to put down our anchors in a beautiful little bay in Eritrea called Lalahab Deset. Finally, finally, finally, we could celebrate leaving the Somali pirates behind.

Although many months of hard slog and excitement lay ahead of us as we made our way up the Red Sea, we knew that the arrival in Eritrea marked the end of the worst part of our journey. The rest would be cruising, although under very windy conditions and in remote and politically unstable areas.

We knew there was still potentially piracy to contend with, but for us this was the "good" kind of piracy, the kind where they just want to rob you, not take you hostage.

We were to remain very tired and nervous for the remainder of the trip. In fact, emotionally it would take months to regain our composure. We are not sure we are over it yet or will ever be. The feeling we were left with was that of a survivor of a horrible accident. There was elation at having made it, but also guilt for surviving where others did not. We felt sad to have put our families through the worry, and angry with ourselves for having put ourselves in that much danger. There was a feeling of wanting to warn others not to attempt this route. There was a need to make others aware of what is going on out there. In short, there were a lot of mixed feelings.

However, that night at Lalahab Deset, we were just happy to be alive and free. That night we all got together on *Serendipity* to have a drink and a laugh, to tell our individual stories, to bring out the guitar, to enjoy the faithful moon and stars above us, and just plain to savour the fact that we were alive and well and the worst was behind us. We would worry about tomorrow ... tomorrow.

CHAPTER 31

When thinking back on that whole awful journey between Thailand and Turkey, Lalahab Deset seems to me to be a dividing point.

There is the time before Lalahab Deset which was the really frightening part for me, the time of constant worry about being captured by the Somali pirates.

And then there is the time after Lalahab Deset, which was easier on me, but harder on Chris. His anxieties about gear failure, heavy weather, and being left behind really came to the fore on the journey up the Red Sea.

When it comes to weather I am an eternal optimist. Whatever happens I know it will get better. When it's nasty, I just go into "endure mode" and wait for better times. As to gear failure . . . well . . . I trust we have a strong boat and . . . I believe that Chris can fix most things. I know . . . not really fair on Chris.

However, I can certainly agree that the Red Sea was not a place where we could easily fix things, nor would we want to be left behind. We still wanted the company of others. If something went wrong there was power in numbers. If we did have a gear problem, maybe someone would have the expertise or the spare part we might need. If there were bandits about, they might leave us alone if we were more than one boat. I suppose that would have been true in some of the other places where we had cruised alone. Somehow it seemed more important now, perhaps just because we were still nervous and tired from the many weeks of worry. We had kind of lost our nerve . . . our confidence.

The Red Sea, specially its southern part, is definitely, at the best of times, pretty much off the beaten track. Very few come here for the pleasure of it. It is an area that the most hardened cruisers might traverse, but only because they have to . . . in order to get somewhere else. I have heard of some cruisers who have chosen to explore the area, but they would be the exception and not the rule.

Having said that . . . and maybe because of that . . . it is also a rewarding place to be. Even if the towns, ragged and dirty and devoid of even minimal comforts, have little to recommend them, there is a stark beauty to the desert landscape, and the water is clear and amazingly turquoise blue, studded with marvellous coral reefs and teeming with fish. In our first anchorage after Lalahab Deset, there was a small shallow lake. Flamingos by the dozen stepped gracefully to and fro, fishing. Flamingos! I had never seen them in the wild! I was struck by the fact that this was Africa! We were sailing along the shores of the African continent. Wow!

And then there is the wind . . . I have never experienced a windier place. It funnels down the Red Sea. And when it hits you . . . it whips up these strange, short, steep waves that are unique to this area. The combined effect is that you are pretty much stopped in your tracks. If the winds are high enough, it is just impossible to proceed to windward.

The trick is to wait for a lull and then proceed with all haste to the next sheltered bay and just hope that you are not caught halfway in between. We had heard stories of boats which had to turn back for many miles, because they could make no progress.

Fortunately, there are lots of places to shelter. There are low-lying sandy islands, not really more than reefs that have popped their head above the water and acquired a covering of desert sand. In places they form a sort of bay, surrounded by desert. They are called *marsas*, and they would provide us with enough shelter to spend a comfortable night at anchor, sheltered from the waves, though not from the howling wind.

Anyway, back there in Lalahab Deset, we contemplated the next thousand miles of challenges facing us in the Red Sea over the next two months and attempted to summon up the inner reserves that would see us through. I have to admit that our inner reserves were at an all-time low. The dial was just above empty. We had been told that if we were lucky, we might have a following wind for some part of the lower half of the Red Sea, but that from about halfway up, it would be a windward struggle all the way. Okie-dokie . . . it had to be done.

As we were now past the pirates, the official convoy started to break up. We had been ten boats in all, from Aden to Lalahab Deset, and some of them now moved on to make their own way up the Red Sea.

Libertad, still in a hurry to get home, left right away. Juan and Lucia were now on their own again. Jeremy had gone aboard *Leah* to help out Gerhardt, as he had lost his American crew member in Aden.

We did have a chance to say goodbye properly to Juan and Lucia, for which I am glad. We had gone through a lot together, and although things had turned a bit pear-shaped in the end, they would still be a part of our lives that we were not likely to forget. We have not stayed in contact, which saddens me, but we did part as friends.

Gerhardt, with Jeremy as crew, left shortly after *Libertad*. They were also in a hurry; Jeremy said he needed to get back to his business, and Gerhardt had family birthdays coming up.

A Brazilian boat that had joined us in Salalah and a German boat that had joined us in Aden also decided to proceed on their own . . . but we did bump into them a couple of times on the way up the coast.

So we were back to six boats: *Serendipity*, the lead boat; the Austrian brothers on *Geliebte*; Penny and Paul on *Bliss*; two French boats which had joined us in Salalah; and us. Chris and I and the Austrian brothers decided that we would like to stay in company with *Serendipity* all the way to Turkey. They were happy for that and Phillip and Lena tried their best to allay our anxieties about the miles ahead.

"It will be hard work, but fun too."

They knew the area and hoped to show us some of the best bits.

And so, we set off some days later up the Eritrean coast. Our first goal was the ancient port town of Massawa.

On the way we had a couple of overnight stops in *marsas* and just as we were approaching the second of these . . . just as we were starting to get into the rhythm of our new cruising ground . . . we were given a reminder that we couldn't let down our guard just yet.

We were now no longer sailing in convoy, just in company, so we had become separated during the day. *Serendipity* was already anchoring and Chris and I were approaching the anchorage, when a call came over the radio. One of the French boats was calling on *Serendipity*, sounding very distressed, saying that they were being boarded by men with machine guns!

Instantly I was back to the knot in the stomach! I just couldn't believe it! Not now! We were supposed to be safe! It was all wrong!

Phillip got on the VHF and tried to calm them down. "Is it a fishing skiff? Are you sure they have guns?"

I could hear that he was hoping that he had misinterpreted their call. They were French. Perhaps a language issue?

No . . . for sure, they repeated that the men had guns and two of them were now on board their boat.

Phillip replied, "I am lifting up my anchor and coming to you . . . Don't worry . . . I will soon be there . . . Give me your position."

I remember thinking what an enormously courageous thing that was for him to do. He had a young wife and crewmember and a baby on board. Yet he was heading over to what might be a pirate skiff, to see if he could help. Me . . . I was horrified, but also secretly thankful that it wasn't us, that we weren't the ones being boarded. Shame on me!

Just a few minutes later, however, the French boat called back to say that the people who had boarded had asked for their passports, looked at the documents, and then gotten back in their skiff and gone away. Phillip guessed that they were local militia, probably looking for a handout. We all breathed a huge sigh of relief!

Perhaps ten minutes later, just as my pulse was getting back to normal, completely without warning, a noise right behind me made me turn around. To my astonishment, there was a skiff with six men in it, already hanging on to our port quarter. I had not even heard them coming.

We had been told that in the case of a pirate attack there is no time to prepare, because they just sneak up on you. Previously I doubted that, but now I knew it to be true, for sure. Chris was just putting away our mainsail and also had not heard a thing.

In the bow of the skiff was a very large, very dark African man in ragged military fatigues who was indicating for me sternly to *"Stop!"*

Behind him another man, dressed in civilian rags, brandished a machine gum which he lifted up to show me in an unmistakeably threatening gesture. There were six of them in total, and only the man in the bows wore any semblance of a uniform. As I had not reacted, he again very firmly said for us to *"Stop!"*

To my later surprise . . . I lost my temper. Completely.

Instead of cowering compliantly, I stood up in the cockpit and shouted, *"No...Do not come near! Go away! No! Go away! Stay away from this boat!"*

Chris turned around to see what the fuss was about and joined me in shouting at them. He indicated with gestures that we would stop and anchor soon and they could come later, when we were anchored.

I continued to shout, *"No . . . Go away!"*

In any case . . . they backed off . . . and left the two of us alone, following at a close distance.

A few minutes later, this performance was repeated.

We were still not at anchor, and we just were not going to stop.

Their leader started to argue with me . . . and the guy with the machine gun kept showing it to me . . . but I just wasn't having it.

I don't know . . . I was not scared at all. Okay . . . I knew that they must be the same guys that had approached the French boat and left . . . but they were still a pretty ominous threat.

In hindsight I don't know what came over me . . . Here were guys with machine guns and I was shooing them away as if they were errant children! I think I had just *had enough* . . . of it all . . . We had run the gauntlet and made it . . . There was just no way I was willing to contemplate anything else. Perhaps the whole experience had hardened me, much more than I had thought.

In the end . . . they could see that they were not going to get any joy out of this crazy woman, so they would either have to act on their threats or leave us alone. Luckily they opted to go.

The experience with the skiff taught us a lesson though. Don't get over-confident. You are still in dangerous waters.

CHAPTER 32

A day later, we arrived in the Port of Massawa and cleared into Eritrea in the shadow of Haile Selassie's bombed out palace.

I think "bombed out" is the appropriate term to apply to the whole of this ancient port town. It has a glorious past and at various times in history has been a bustling, important harbour. You can still see remnants of its former glory in the once-elegant buildings that lined the Port.

Today, however, all is crumbling, returning to the dust. The buildings are mostly ruins, pockmarked with bullet holes, the streets unpaved, and the houses ragged hovels. I grew up in India, so am no stranger to poverty . . . but Eritrea was the poorest place I have ever seen. It is a Christian country, surrounded by Muslim neighbours, and is said to be at war with every one of them. To this end, everyone, men and women, boys and girls alike, have to do their stint in the army. We were told that you could only leave the army when they decided to let you go . . . if you were a boy . . . and only upon getting married or pregnant . . . if you were a girl. Thus commerce and ambition are stifled, and there seems no way out of the cycle of poverty.

And yet . . . here is the "but" . . . the people of Eritrea are a proud and noble people. They are tall and graceful, and though dark-skinned, are very fine-featured. They really are extraordinarily beautiful. And, as is often the case with people who have nothing, they were generous with what little they had.

We were invited for coffee by a local family. You could see that they had once been quite affluent. They still owned their own two-story home. It had not seen any maintenance for a very long time and was falling down around them. From this crumbling building they brought out a couple of plastic chairs into the dirt road, and then went to neighbours to borrow a couple more. From somewhere a small wooden table was found and set up with a scrap of rag and decorated with some green leaves . . . the leaves being luxuries in themselves, as this was a barren, dusty place.

The oldest daughter of the family was the official "coffee maker." She sat on a wooden stool in front of a small brazier. First she poured a handful of fresh coffee beans into her hand and inspected each one for defects. Next she placed them in a small roasting pan and roasted them over the hot coals, releasing the most heavenly aroma! Once roasted to her satisfaction, the beans were placed in a clay mortar and pestle and crushed. Next the grounds were inserted, with water, in a vase-shaped earthenware vessel with a thin pouring spout. This she placed directly on the hot coals to brew the coffee.

In the meantime her mother produced a small nugget of frankincense which she lit in an incense burner to provide a pleasant smell and placed it and some tiny coffee-cups on a tray.

Once the coffee was brewed, a small plug of loose vegetable fibres was placed in the spout of the "coffee pot" as a sort of filter, and the finished product was poured into the tiny coffee cups.

The whole process had taken almost an hour, but it was definitely the best cup of coffee I have ever tasted. The enjoyment of it was over in an instant, and it seemed to us Westerners a longwinded way to go about it. But there are lessons to be learned here. What was on offer was far more than the coffee, although this in itself must have been a precious and luxurious commodity for that family. They gave us of their time, their respect, their hospitality. We were treated as honoured guests, and that was the real gift. I left feeling humbled and acutely aware of the financial gulf between us and them.

Chris and I have always carried some inexpensive items like T-shirts and caps as gifts for the locals, but this time I went back to the boat and pulled out all my own clothes from the closet, to see what I could give them. I returned with wrapped parcels of jackets, blouses, and skirts as well as our only teapot and matching cups.

Meg, the young American girl, who was crew on *Serendipity*, was about the same age as the daughter who had made the coffee. She decided to invite her to accompany us to the only semi-decent restaurant in town that evening.

It was obvious that this young Eritrean girl had pulled out all the stops to dress up for the occasion and also obvious that she had never set foot inside a restaurant before. Meg tried to make her comfortable, but even so, she would not eat inside the restaurant, indicating she was ashamed, and chose to eat outside. Meg stayed with her.

Later, they went on to a bar, and her new local friend insisted that she wanted to buy Meg a beer. The purpose of the evening was for Meg to treat her, and not the other way around, but Meg understood . . . This was a proud young girl and she needed to do this . . . even if she spent money she did not have.

At the end of our stay in Massawa, Meg gave her all her remaining Eritrean currency, saying it would not be any good to her at our next stop. She took some convincing to accept. It was considerably more than the price of that beer, and her new friend struggled to stem the tears that came unwanted at this generous gift. It was small change for Meg . . . a fortune to her.

A proud and beautiful people.

On the advice of Phillip and Lena, we also took the opportunity to visit the capital of Eritrea, the city of Asmara, high up in the hills.

I have mentioned before that one of my favourite aspects of the cruising life is the contrasts it brings. Asmara was very different from Massawa. One would hardly believe we were still in the same country, or even the same continent. Though I would not describe it as a wealthy place, it nonetheless retained the character of a Mediterranean town, with cobbled streets and sidewalk cafés, with cathedrals and small quaint market squares. Eritrea was once an Italian colony, and here was the proof of it. It was also obvious that the citizens were proud of their "European" heritage. Dark-skinned gentlemen in their once elegant, but now shabby, three piece suits, hats obligatory, inhabited the sidewalk cafés and inquired (in fluent Italian) where we hailed from.

On the way back in the minibus, we stopped at a small restaurant for a quick coffee. I took myself off to the ladies facilities and there was a bit of a queue. Two beautifully, elegantly dressed, jewellery bedecked, black-skinned ladies waited alongside me and I could not help commenting on their finery. In particular I admired a large interestingly shaped gold-plated ring that one of them wore.

When I came out of the loo, this lady stopped me and took off her ring and put it on my finger. When I tried to hand it back to her, she insisted that it was a gift and no amount of protest from me would make her change her mind. Her husband soon joined her and in broken English he explained that they were from the Sudan, newlyweds, on their honeymoon. He also insisted that I keep the ring.

Later, I was told that in Arab countries you must be very careful not to admire the possessions of others, because they then feel a moral obligation to gift you that item. To refuse would be an insult. It was a good lesson. I vowed to be more careful in future. However, I will always treasure that ring.

Soon it was time to move on. *Serendipity* had once more attempted to get a proper repair to their gearbox, but unfortunately we were still in too remote a place to obtain the right parts. Phillip, with the help of the Austrian brothers, who had been Porsche mechanics in their pre-cruising existence, did their best to effect a usable repair. Maybe they would be able to make a more permanent job of it in the Sudan, the next country up the coast.

We left Eritrea with the feeling that we had seen something special. It is hardly a place that you would visit as a Westerner without a very good reason. And yet, there is beauty there too: in the people, in the mountains, in its proud history.

CHAPTER 33

Eritrea, Asmara, the Sudan . . . doesn't it all sound incredibly exotic?! Even this battle-hardened and weary soul could not help feeling a little excited at passing through these historic and remote places. In our travels, we have been fortunate enough to be able to visit quite a few places that most have never heard of before. These, however, were names from our school days . . . names from the history books. And I suppose I had never really thought they would be places that I would visit.

The sail from Massawa to Suakin in the Sudan took us six days. The name of the game was "dodge the wind." The prevailing pattern seemed to be that the wind would kick up with force in the late morning or early afternoon. So we up-anchored at first light, to make some miles while we could.

On one occasion, we only managed ten miles, before we were faced with thirty knots of headwinds and those short steep seas that make progress just about impossible. Fortunately there was a hole-in-a-reef anchorage nearby . . . not recommended in the guidebooks . . . but better than going backwards . . . and we spent an uncomfortable night there, being buffeted by the winds.

For the most part, however, we did manage to sneak into a *marsa*: those lovely desert-bordered bays with their low-lying barrier islands.

These were trying times for Chris, with his weather anxieties. He worried ceaselessly about gear failure, and although we now had the luxury of being at anchor most nights, he was unable to sleep with the wind howling around his ears. I could see him deteriorating physically before my eyes. He is such a healthy, positive chap normally, but this was taking a terrible toll on him. He had dark circles under his eyes for lack of sleep and complained of stomach pains. Sometimes his worries were not rational . . . and he knew it . . . Nevertheless I could not "talk him down," and I worried for his health.

Phillip and Lena were lovely. They had noticed his struggles, and did their best to allay his fears. Phillip went out of his way to stay in close touch on the VHF and to assure Chris that he would not lead us into any winds that we could not handle . . . nor would he leave any boat behind. He often came over to *Skylark II*, when we were at anchor, to discuss the next passage with Chris . . . and I know that he singled us out for these chats. They really were a comfort to Chris and he always felt better when Phillip had been for a visit.

Chris also sought out Lena, who was a therapist in her pre-boating existence, and tried to get to the bottom of his anxieties. She prescribed some sleeping pills, which we were able to obtain in the Sudan. As we still had many miles of the same trials to get through, this was not the time for any in-depth reflections on childhood causes of anxiety. The most important thing, to her mind, was that he should catch up on his sleep.

At this stage, we were still in a mini-convoy of six boats. *Serendipity*, *Geliebte*, the two French boats, *Bliss*, and us. Though it was a physically demanding time from a sailing perspective, we also had some wonderful times, sharing meals and Happy Hours among our little fleet. One evening we had a picnic and a fire on a beach. Quite often we met for a sing-along in the cockpit of *Serendipity*.

We really got to know each other on this leg, and having been through tough times together, there was that incredible bond of diverse people with a common experience. It really felt like we were a sort of family as we slowly got to know one another's foibles, things both positive and negative, and quickly accepted them. We were different ages, from different countries and cultures, had different mother tongues, and hailed from different levels of society . . . but it mattered not one bit. We were in this together and were enhanced by each other's company.

Heavy weather notwithstanding, it was a magical time for our little fleet. But we knew it would soon come to an end, as the French boats and *Bliss* were in a hurry and were already talking of continuing northwards at a more rapid pace than the rest of us.

Finally, we arrived in Suakin, a small port south of the much larger commercial port of Port Sudan.

Suakin can best be described as biblical, though it is decidedly Muslim. When I say biblical, I mean that not much seems to have changed there since the time of the Bible stories. The buildings were mostly built with coral rocks and have over the centuries slowly and gently reverted to piles of coral rubble. The older part of the town looks like a bomb site, with only the minarets of the mosques and a few doorways remaining standing. No one seems in the least bit inclined to clean up the place either, perhaps accustomed to living among the dust and rubble. Donkeys pulling wooden carts laden with water butts slowly trundled along the dusty lanes, and turban and fez-clad gentlemen in flowing robes, often carrying a sword, lounged lazily in filthy coffee shops. There were not many women to be seen, but we did catch glimpses of them early in the morning, trying to wash in the sea, encumbered by long gowns and veils. There was also a prison near the harbour, and we saw convicts under guard collecting seawater, presumably to flush latrines in the medieval-looking high-walled windowless enclosure where they spent their days. I shuddered to think what conditions might be like behind those walls!

While we were in the Sudan, there was an incident that to me demonstrated the strength of character of our leader Phillip.

Now, I don't want to paint Phillip out to be any kind of saint, because he was not. In fact, I would describe him as a difficult man, quick to temper, and extremely demanding of those around him. He did not suffer fools gladly and expected no less than perfection from his crew. There were times when both his young American crew, Meg, and his wife Lena, sought a quiet cup of tea and a chat on *Skylark II*, when they had invoked his fury. Phillip, it seemed to me, saw life in black and white; there were no grey areas, and he had no compromise in him when things were wrong to his eyes.

Such a time occurred when we were returning in a minibus after a shopping trip to Port Sudan.

We saw a very large herd of camels, maybe a hundred of them. The camel herders were themselves mounted on camels, swords tucked into their saddles. It was a great photo opportunity, so we stopped the bus and mingled with the herd.

We were just returning to our bus when the camel herders decided to take the herd over the busy road to the other side. I suppose drivers in the Sudan are used to this kind of thing and generally stop and wait for the herd to have crossed the road.

However, in the distance we noticed a large articulated lorry with a trailer coming toward the camels (and us) at a very high speed. This was a huge vehicle . . . like a Mack truck. He showed no signs at all of slowing down.

Phillip was almost at the minibus and reacted immediately, shouting to us to get away from the bus . . . away from the road.

An instant later, the truck ploughed into the unsuspecting camels.

Bang! Bang! Bang!

It was a horrible sound and the aftermath was worse. There were several dead and dying camels in the road, camels braying, screaming in their death-throes, camel herders shouting . . . It was awful.

In the meantime the truck, though slowed by the collision with the camels, nonetheless got back on the road and continued on.

Now Phillip was shouting at us to get into the bus immediately. I remember thinking that this was wise. Previous experience in this kind of situation had taught me that often the blame would fall on the foreigners . . . even though we had nothing to do with this whatsoever. Tempers would undoubtedly flare and we could get caught in the crossfire. So I jumped into the bus very quickly, as did the others.

However, getting away was not Phillip's intention at all. The camel herders had been wronged and he was not going to let the truck driver get away with it. He urged the driver of the minibus to catch up with the truck and pass it. Despite the vehement protests of the driver, he made him pull over and got out, standing in the road in front of the oncoming truck.

He picked up a stone and threatened to throw it, all the while shouting to the truck driver to *"Stop!"*

It was a real David and Goliath situation . . . Phillip with his rock in hand . . . no thought for his own safety . . . and this enormous truck which could easily run him over and barely notice it.

Miraculously, the truck stopped. The driver got out with a sheepish grin and nearly fell over. He was obviously drunk. Phillip continued to threaten him and shout at him until one of the owners of the camel herd showed up. As soon as Phillip saw them arrive, he got us all back into the minibus and we took off.

On the way home, we were stopped at a roadblock and pulled over. The police wanted a bribe to let us carry on.

It was not a good time to be asking Phillip for a bribe. He was still full of adrenaline from the camel incident and yet again was not going to compromise his principles.

He got out of the minibus, found the head honcho, and told him in no uncertain terms that he was not getting a bribe out of us. He felt we had no reason to pay.

"Why are you charging us?! . . . Because of our white faces?!" he said.

The rest of us in the bus kind of cringed and would have been happy to part with the twenty dollars they wanted . . . but not Phillip. Faced with this uncompromising white guy, the authorities backed down, and we were sent on our way without a bribe.

To me, these incidents were indicative of Phillip's strong personal sense of fair play. I have to admire a guy who stands up for right and wrong, no matter what. He is a larger than life character for sure, and no doubt rubs some people the wrong way, but we felt lucky to be in his care. His strength in uncertain times carried us through, and Chris and I are grateful and feel that we would not have made it through those harrowing times without him.

CHAPTER 34

We were now roughly halfway up the Red Sea, in the half where we could expect only winds from the bow. We could also expect these winds to get stronger as we proceeded further north. In other words, from a sailing point of view, it would get more and more challenging.

We were about to depart from Suakin, when the skipper on *Geliebte,* one of the Austrian brothers, fell ill. What we first thought was a touch of flu turned more serious, and he developed a high fever and problems with his kidneys.

Our doctors, Penny and Paul on *Bliss*, had unfortunately departed a few days earlier to carry on northwards on their own. It was not the kind of place where you go and find a local GP, so we tried to get advice from Penny and Paul over the radio. His brother also managed to communicate with the family doctor in Austria, but of course, there is only so much you can do over the phone and radio.

We decided to wait it out and see if he got better. The days went by, and he was, if anything, worse, even starting to hallucinate on occasion. It was again a reminder of how vulnerable you are in remote places like that.

Phillip resolutely stuck to his word, that no one would be left behind. The French boats had also left a few days earlier, so it was *Skylark II*, *Serendipity*, and *Geliebte*, all waiting for Franz to get better.

The problem was not just to get him safely to adequate medical care, but his departure would have meant having to leave *Geliebte* on her own in an unsafe environment, as his brother would be unable to sail her to the Med by himself. Who knows what would have been left of the boat after a couple of months unattended in Suakin?!

In the end, just as we were about to arrange transport home for Franz, he did rally enough for us to carry on.

The solution was to transfer young Meg from *Serendipity* to *Geliebte* as crew, to help brother Hans to sail the boat. This turned out to be a baptism of fire for Meg. It seems that Hans, though competent crew, had never skippered his brother's boat. He felt out of his depth, and it ended up being Meg in command. She in turn had never had much to do with boating before joining *Serendipity* a year and a half earlier, and had certainly never skippered a boat.

I take my hat off to her. She is one tough young lady. She confessed later that she was scared to death, but she rose to the challenge.

Meg, then in her early twenties, had grown up on a large ranch in the States; in fact she herself owned a couple of herds of cattle . . . a real cowgirl. Though that does not prepare you to skipper a boat in challenging water, it did, it seems, provide her with the common sense and the grit required to pull it off. Go Meg!

We carried on northward. We could not avoid the wind much now, though we still looked for lulls. However, we did try to stay as close to the western shore as possible, tacking back and forth in a narrow strip of sea, in between the reefs that line the coast and the reefs and barrier islands that run parallel with it. There was perhaps only a couple of miles of sea room between the reefs, so we all did our very best to sail as close to the wind as possible and to delay our tacks until we were practically kissing the reef-edge with our bows.

For Chris and me it was a constant struggle to keep up. *Skylark II* is a blue water cruising boat, built more for comfort than speed. She is not a slug, and we are mostly very happy with her performance, but she was no competition for the much larger, sleeker *Serendipity*. Nor could she match the performance of *Geliebte*, a racing boat which throughout had been one of the best performers in the convoy.

So we motor-sailed all the time, using our auxiliary engine to boost our speed and ability to stay close to the wind.

The silver lining to this particular cloud was that we improved our sailing skills quite a bit. We had been pretty casual sailors before now. We learned to tweak and pull and adjust constantly, to get every last inch of performance out of our boat.

It was another week of challenging sailing and beautiful nights in uninhabited *marsas*.

We now bonded even more, with just the three boats together. We became family. Phillip and Lena were Mum and dad, Meg was the elder daughter, the Austrian brothers were the uncles, and Chris and I the grandparents. And baby Isla . . . she was the star! When we had first met Phillip and Lena in Langkawi, she had been a baby in diapers, still rounded with baby fat and speaking only a couple of words. She had grown up in front of our eyes.

Six months later, she was now turning into a beautiful, confident little girl, who knew us all by name (and boat name) and could converse with us in Dutch, English, or German, depending on who she was talking to. All of us took turns babysitting her on our boats to give her parents a break, and we were the ones who benefited from that. Just a lovely touch of normalcy in what was still a difficult time.

Serendipity was still plagued with problems with her gearbox and now also had issues with an in-mast roller furling system.

Phillip just couldn't believe it. It was he who had carefully vetted each yacht before they were allowed to join the convoy, to make sure they would be up to it. He, more than anyone, knew how rigorous this journey would be. The boats needed to be in really good shape to manage it. *Serendipity* had been checked and re-checked . . . and still . . . it was his boat that ended up having ongoing problems. If we had been anywhere with decent marine stores or decent mechanics, the problem would long ago have been taken care of. As even the most basic facilities eluded us, Phillip had tried one "jury-rig" after another to make a temporary fix which would enable them to carry on. I think a lesser man would have given up by now. It is a credit to Phillip, and the Austrian brothers who helped him a lot, that *Serendipity* was able to complete the journey without major delays.

In the meantime, *Geliebte* was also starting to show signs of trouble. Just as we were approaching the reef entrance to one of the *marsas*, her engine quit. Now it was *Serendipity* towing *Geliebte*. Franz and Hans got the engine going again and that evening we tried to make light of it. We renamed our convoy the "Tow-to-Turkey" convoy!

Two days short of Port Ghalib, the entry port for Egypt, there was another mishap. In trying to fix their roller-furling issues while underway, Phillip's thumb had been badly crushed when the entire weight of the sail and roller furler collapsed on his hand. He was in terrible pain and naturally very worried about possible lasting damage to his thumb. All Lena and Meg could do was to wrap it up in bandages and give him morphine. Luckily, there was a decent hospital in Port Ghalib, and he was able to have it seen to immediately upon our arrival there. Thankfully, there would be no permanent damage.

Port Ghalib was an oasis of luxury in the middle of the desert. There was a modern marina, albeit almost completely empty of boats. Beautiful holiday homes, also mostly empty, lined the artificial canals of the marina complex. Empty, luxurious cafés, restaurants, and shops completed the picture. This was the first manifestation of what would become typical for Egypt. There were two worlds, one for the locals and one for the tourists and the wealthy.

We did get a glimpse of the "real Egypt" a few days later, in the small, sleepy port of El Quseir. No luxury hotels here, just a somewhat dirty beach with ramshackle shelters on it, where one could join the locals in lazing over a cup of coffee or smoking a water-pipe.

In El Quseir, life caught up with us yet again. Just to make sure that we would never ever forget the year 2011, with its trials and tribulations, we got the news that Chris' father, Sid, had died. He had made it to ninety-five, and enjoyed most of those years, so . . . as they say . . . "He had a good innings," but it was still a shock to know he was gone. Ironically, one of the reasons why this journey had been attempted was to be closer to the UK to enable us to spend more time with Chris' dad.

Again, Phillip stuck to his promise of not leaving anyone behind. He suggested we all proceed to the next decent marina in Abu Tig, and assured us that *Serendipity* and *Geliebte* would wait for us there while we flew back to the UK to attend the funeral. We were very grateful.

Our week in the UK had its own challenges. Apart from the sadness surrounding this family get-together, while we were there our email account was stolen by scammers. They got hold of our contacts list, locked us out of our account, and sent an email to all our contacts indicating that we had been robbed and assaulted and desperately needed money. We could not warn anyone, as we could not get into our account. We had a list of contacts on the boat in Egypt and Meg and Lena retrieved it from *Skylark II* and faxed it to us. Sadly, by the time we were able to warn our friends of the scam, three had already sent money, one of them 1,400 Euros!

We also had to cancel all our credit and debit cards, as there was information about them within our personal emails. As there was no fixed address to which the banks could send new cards, we would have to manage with cash only for the remainder of the journey. Needless to say, we needed these problems like a hole in the head!

In any case, we got back to the boat in Egypt and left Abu Tig just hours later, as the others were now anxious to get on.

The route took us across to the eastern shore of the Red Sea, skirting the Sinai Peninsula. Here the Red Sea narrows into the Gulf of Suez, creating even more of a wind funnel. Again it was a question of waiting for lulls, but these were now fewer and farther between. The French boats who were a bit ahead of us reported that they had made several attempts to get out of a certain bay and had to abort twice before succeeding to make headway on the third attempt.

So . . . there was a lot of waiting around. We made the best of it, and even managed to get in a visit to the ancient monastery of St. Catherine, which is at the foot of Mount Sinai and constructed on the very spot where Moses saw the burning bush. The monastery has always been considered a very holy place and has never been razed or attacked. Even Mohammed is said to have visited the site and declared it exempt from pillage.

In any case, we finally arrived in the Port of Suez.

Here we had to take on an Egyptian pilot. He would stay on board until Ismailia. The next day a second pilot would take us to Port Said, the entrance to the Mediterranean.

We had heard all sorts of horror stories about these Egyptian pilots. We were told to expect to be hassled constantly for *baksheesh* (a tip or bribe). In fact, the advice was to put twenty one dollar bills in an envelope and show it to the pilot when he stepped on board. We should tell him that every time he hassled us or annoyed us in any way, we would remove a dollar from the envelope.

We did prepare our envelopes . . . but . . . for whatever reason . . . our experience turned out to be completely different. We never did give them the speech about the envelope, and despite this, both our pilots were lovely chaps and never asked for a thing. They were grateful for the lunch we served and never mentioned *baksheesh* once. In fact, in both cases, we had to hand them the envelope unasked for, at the end of the trip.

As a parting shot to end our Red Sea adventure, we did still have one small spot of trouble at Port Said. We had already cleared out of Egypt in Port Suez and been told by the authorities there that that would suffice. On arrival at Port Said we could proceed immediately into the Med, they had assured us.

However, I guess the authorities in Port Said wanted a piece of the action, so they were indicating to us that we had to come into the marina and clear out again . . . agent fees . . . marina fees . . . etc.

Once more, Phillip was having none of it. He told Franz, Hans, and us, that we were absolutely not to go into the marina, so we circled around while Phillip engaged in a heated discussion with the authorities. He insisted that we were already cleared out of the country and that if we went into the marina we would have to again clear into Egypt. The authorities insisted that we could not leave without being checked again by Customs. It was a stalemate.

In the end, the authorities had to give in as Phillip was obviously not going to see it their way. The solution was to send out a boat with a Customs official, who took some details from each boat (probably to save face), and then told us we could leave.

We turned our bows northward . . . and with soaring hearts . . . left the Red Sea behind and entered the Mediterranean!

To get here we had traversed more than six thousand miles of water, almost all of it challenging. We had been worried and tired for six long months. We had put over a thousand hours on the engine. We had been lucky to pass unscathed through pirates, escape arrest in India, dodge the worst of the political unrests, and avoid gear breakages and reefs.

Looking back, we asked ourselves whether we had been brave or foolish to attempt this. For us . . . the answer is clear . . . we had been foolish. We both strongly feel that had we known then . . . back there in Thailand . . . what we know now . . . there is no way that we would ever have chosen this route. If we had it to do again, if we could turn the clock back . . . we would have chosen the South Africa route.

Now, I know that other boats who traversed the Indian Ocean and the Red Sea in the same year as us feel that it was okay; it was not so bad. Even one couple who were in our convoy feel that way. I have even heard some say they would do it again.

To my mind with no disrespect intended . . . everyone is entitled to their opinion . . . this is dangerous talk. Of course, if you were not hassled, not even once. If you did not have any encounters with pirates or armed skiffs. If you sailed straight through the Red Sea and never landed in the politically troubled areas. Sure . . . it might seem to you like just any other cruising journey, albeit with more headwinds.

But the fact remains that the only reason you got through is that you were lucky. It is absolutely not true that the pirates don't target yachts. They will take anything they stumble across. And if you are among the unlucky . . . the consequences are horrific. Think of the murdered crew of *Quest*. Ask the Danish family who endured horrors in captivity for many long months. Ask them if it is worth the risk! Are you really willing to gamble your lives and those of your loved ones on the chance that you will be lucky?!

My advice to anyone who reads this is . . . go another way . . . or transport your boat! Please!

CHAPTER 35

But that day . . . we the lucky ones . . . made our way toward Cyprus.

It was an incredible feeling to have Mediterranean waters under our keel! Our minds had for so long been reaching out for this. I never could have imagined that it would mean so much to me. I had always loved the Med, having sailed there in my twenties. But this was now no longer just another sea. It represented security, a familiar environment, a freedom from the worries of the last few months. We felt released.

There was also a feeling of freedom from having to travel in convoy, to struggle to keep up with the others.

To celebrate, Chris and I immediately turned the engine off. We wanted to sail, to sail at our own pace, to choose our own course, to sail alone. Wow! The freedom in that!

We told *Serendipity* and *Geliebte* not to wait for us. "We will see you in Cyprus in a couple of days!"

Life, being life . . . buts and all . . . the forecast beam winds did not eventuate and the wind again was from the bows. We tacked and tacked and tacked back and forth, dodging all the many ships waiting to enter the Suez Canal.

By nightfall we did not seem to have come very far from the shores of Egypt, so reluctantly the engine was turned on again.

But nothing could diminish the wonderful elation we felt.

I remember sitting in the cockpit and being struck by a surge of emotion. We have made it, we have truly made it!

I don't think I fully realized until then that even I, who was always able to think ahead to better times, had started to wonder whether we would ever emerge from that quagmire of piracy, strong winds, and political unrest.

But here we were. And within easy reach, we now had so many wonderful countries and cultures to explore. After the distances that we had just put behind us, Spain, France, Italy, Greece, Turkey, and more were all mere days away.

I felt my curiosity and excitement surge. I turned to Chris to share my excitement with him.

Poor Chris . . . he looked back at me with tired eyes that said it all. "Desi, let's just get to Turkey!"

And he was right. What we wanted most of all at that moment was to get to somewhere, put our anchor down and just rest. There would be time for exploration later. Now, we and *Skylark II* deserved a well-earned break.

On the very last leg from Cyprus to Turkey, we ended up, by choice, sailing together with *Serendipity* and *Geliebte*. Much as we were enjoying our newfound freedom, it was hard to break those bonds. An elated Phillip now took on the role of tour guide and wanted to show us his favourite spots from his last stay in Turkey three years before.

As we approached the Turkish coast, we all pulled out our signal flags and hoisted them up the mast. Finally, finally, the Thailand to Turkey journey was over.

Slowly, over the next few weeks I could feel my old confidence returning. Despite the rigors of that last journey, it was but six months of hardship in now almost six years of cruising. Now, the sun was shining. We had our health, we had food on the table, and we had our beloved *Skylark*, a floating home that would take us on new adventures whenever we felt ready. All around us, centuries of history lay waiting for us to discover.

What followed was a lovely few weeks of cruising up the Turkish coast, still in company with *Serendipity* and *Geliebte*. Eventually the bonds started to dissolve and we all made separate plans for the coming winter.

As for Chris and I . . . we have spent a wonderful, quiet, and calm winter on our boat in the beautiful, sleepy, ancient village of Ucagiz on the Lycian coast of Turkey.

There are 350 villagers here and the few yachts that are moored to the town dock have all been left by their owners for the winter. Chris and I are the only foreigners and are privileged to be incorporated into village life.

Chris has made himself into an unofficial dock master and is trying to lead the locals by example by picking up litter on the roadsides as he goes for his daily walk up the hill.

I have been invited to join the local women's weekly prayer group and joint lunch. Though not a Muslim, I have learned to tie on a headscarf in the Turkish way and spent many happy hours sharing lunch and a few words of stumbling Turkish with "the girls."

It is a perfect time for us. Slowly the stresses of our sail from Thailand are dissolving and we have started to look ahead to new adventures, though of a gentler kind.

This is where I will end my narrative . . . with Chris and I having Sunday breakfast in the cockpit with the beautiful views of Kekova Bay all around us. Soon we will leave here and explore more of Turkey and then . . . perhaps . . . Greece. Life is peaceful and . . . We are safe again.

We still love the life. We are still in awe and humbled by how lucky we are. Life has certainly thrown some challenges our way. But in the end, neither lack of finance, nor alcoholism, nor cancer, nor Somali pirates have succeeded in stopping us from fulfilling our dream.

It was a harrowing journey, but we have made it, and the path ahead looks full of promise.

On board *Skylark II*, Uçagiz, the 18th of March, 2012.

ABOUT THE AUTHOR

Desiree Trattles was born in Sweden. At five years of age, she moved with her family to Calcutta, India. She attended boarding school in the Himalayas, studied art in Brazil, and economics in Sweden. In her adult life she was a tour guide in Ibiza, Sri Lanka, and the Canary Islands, painted catamarans on a beach in the Caribbean, delivered sailboats up and down the East Coast of the U.S, etc. In her mid-thirties, she and husband Chris moved to New Zealand. They lived in Paraparaumu and after going back to University to take an Accountancy Degree, Desiree worked in Wellington as a chartered accountant for one of the "Big Five" firms.

Sailing has always been Desiree's great passion and in 2007, she and her husband left New Zealand to follow their dreams and sail the world in their small yacht, *Skylark II*. They are still living on their boat, currently in Sicily. *A Harrowing Journey* is Desiree's first book.

11738485R00111

Printed in Great Britain
by Amazon.co.uk, Ltd.,
Marston Gate.